Neal Alexander AInstAM(Dip) grew up in Burnley, Lancashire and is a military veteran and an Incorporated Administrator.

Neal served for 27 years in the army and is now semi-retired and resides in Germany with his wife, Marion.

Attaining the rank of Warrant Officer Class Two in the army and serving in Germany, Northern Ireland, Canada, Kenya, Bosnia, Poland, Kosovo and Cyprus. Neal escorted the Queen and the Duke of Edinburgh on their state visit to Germany in 2004. He was awarded an International Diploma in Administrative Management and a Diploma in German.

A retired cross-country champion (in a team) who ran many half and 2 full marathons (London and Berlin) and is now a marathon cyclist, an avid artist of over 100 exhibits and an accomplished poet.

To all those who read this book of poems, thank you for giving my words a chance.

To my wife, Marion, and our children—Vanessa, Matthew and Hannah: thank you for your love and support over the years, I could not have done this without you. Marion was my soundboard throughout putting this together, bless her.

In memory of my mother and father who both passed away in 2018, thank you for believing in me and guiding me in the right direction. Dad, thank you for the laughs, and Mum, thank you for beating me in every game of Scrabble.

For lost friends, you may not be by my side anymore, but you will always be on my mind and in my heart.

Neal Alexander

Life, an Extraordinary Journey

AUSTIN MACAULEY PUBLISHERS®
LONDON * CAMBRIDGE * NEW YORK * SHARJAH

Copyright © Neal Alexander 2026

The right of Neal Alexander to be identified as author of this work has been asserted by the author in accordance with sections 77 and 78 of the Copyright, Designs and Patents Act 1988.

All rights reserved. No part of this publication may be reproduced, stored in a retrieval system, or transmitted in any form or by any means, electronic, mechanical, photocopying, recording, or otherwise, without the prior permission of the publishers.

The story, experiences, and words are the author's alone.

Any person who commits any unauthorised act in relation to this publication may be liable to criminal prosecution and civil claims for damages.

A CIP catalogue record for this title is available from the British Library.

ISBN 9781035875900 (Paperback)
ISBN 9781035875917 (ePub e-book)

www.austinmacauley.com

First Published 2026
Austin Macauley Publishers Ltd®
1 Canada Square
Canary Wharf
London
E14 5AA

This endeavour would not have been possible without the memories. That is to say, that I am deeply indebted to my wife, Marion, and our children, Vanessa, Matthew and Hannah. Your memories complete me and thank you for your love, support, patience and sacrifices. You were pushed from pillar to post with your varied moves and schools.

On behalf of Marion and I and especially our children, we are deeply indebted to Service Children's Education British Forces Germany, St. George's – The British International School Köln and Cambridge International School Berlin. Thank you very much.

I could not have undertaken this journey without Her[1] Majesty's Armed Forces, well they did take me in after all. The truth is, if you give the army your all, you will indeed enjoy an illustrious career, well that was my case anyway. It gave me direction; it educated me and it allowed me to have countless opportunities.

Thank you to 'Google' for some memory recaps!

The front and back covers and the blurb were inspired by Marion and Hannah.

---

[1] In my case.

Table of Contents

Preface	11
1. Pre-Adolescence (Part 1 of 4)	13
2. Teenager (Part 2 of 4)	17
3. Leaving Home (Part 3 of 4)	21
4. Finding MY Way (Part 4 of 4)	24
5. Boot Camp	26
6. Deutschland (German, Germany in English)	32
7. Canucks	37
8. Slipper City	44
9. Hochzeit (German, Wedding in English)	51
10. Straight Shooter	60
11. It's a Boy	62
12. Cold War	71
13. On Safari	85
14. Marathon Man	89
15. Being In/Complete	97
16. Balkans Calling	106
17. Lost Friends	120
18. Day Trip to Egypt	128
19. Köln (German, Cologne in English)	134
20. Highpoint	140
21. Adult Education	144

22. Military Veteran	**151**
23. Civvy Street	**160**
24. Military Medals	**164**
25. Remembrance (Another Synonym)	**168**
Word Search	*171*
Words to Find	*171*
Word Search (Solution)	*172*
26. Pets IV	**173**
27. Shooting Stars	**180**
28. Role Reversal	**182**
29. Regrets	**185**
30. Family, A Short Story	**189**
Epilogue	**191**

Preface

I am a British army veteran and live in Germany with my German wife, Marion and we have been married for 36 years. We have three (adult) children; our 2 daughters, Vanessa and Hannah, live here in Germany and our son Matthew lives in the UK. We have 2 grandchildren—Liah and Ayden.

The first poem I wrote was actually the last one in this series; this poem inspired me to go back in time and start from the beginning. The poems are basically my life journey that takes me from about 9 years old to the present day. Therefore, the poems are practically in a chronological order of life events. The poems intertwine with each other but I believe the majority of them can also stand alone. In short, I had an average childhood; unfortunately, my parents separated when I was 9, when we lived with just our dad. I embarrassingly left high school with nothing, but with no one else to blame but myself. At school, I did not really take part in many sports apart from probably the compulsory sports days. You could say that I escaped my late teen life when I probably, abruptly, joined the army.

The army however was the best move I made. My life really started after joining the army. I spent nearly 27 years serving the Crown and served mainly in Germany (including Berlin (twice) and Köln (Cologne)). From Germany, I deployed on operations and exercises (chronologically) in Canada, Northern Ireland, Kenya, Bosnia, Kosovo, Poland and Cyprus. I enlisted as an infantry soldier and later transferred to administration about halfway through my military career. I am extremely proud of my personal achievements and my military medals. I was awarded an International Diploma in Administrative Management and proudly passed O-Level (equivalent) English and Maths and A-Level (equivalent) German—all at the age of 40+.

I have many running medals; I was a Corps and Regimental Cross-Country runner and I particularly boast 2 full marathon medals (London and Berlin), 25km marathon medal (Berlin) and several half-marathon medals. I also participated in many cycling expeditions and marathons in Canada, Switzerland and Germany (mostly the Mosel River region). The highpoint of my military career was being selected to work at the British Embassy in Berlin, a high-profile and prestigious post. There, I met many famous faces, including members of the royal family, and I have had the pleasure of escorting the Queen and the Duke of Edinburgh on their state visit to Germany in 2004.

I had my first *real* civilian job at 48 years old and I am semi-retired now. My hobbies include walking, cycling, generally keeping fit and I am an avid artist and like to paint or create pieces of art as gifts for family and friends. My new passion is poetry. We role-reversed at home and I was promoted to househusband. Sadly, I was orphaned just before my 54th birthday but am grateful that my parents lived for nearly 2 centuries between them. I was lucky in a way as my wife Marion lost her brother when she was 18 months old, her mother when she was 9 and her father when she was 16.

I enjoyed putting these poems (with their illustrations) together, they sort of reminded me of who I am and it helped me rekindle some great (and some sad, bad and/or challenging) memories. I have purposely omitted surnames of people to protect their identities.

Life really is a rollercoaster.

Neal Alexander

1. Pre-Adolescence (Part 1 of 4)

Probably an earlier memory than 9, not sure; often shaving with my dad,
I would sit on the toilet seat and he would say "you shave like this, lad."
He would give me one of his razors with the cover on it and a bit of cream,
He would then go to work in the small hours and I would go back to a dream.

I remember Sunday dinner with the whole family and not liking vegetables,
Mum made good food; I am sure she encouraged us to eat those edibles.
My oldest brother Steve left home to play in an army band and become a soldier,
He went to Ulster; I thought it was a foreign land far, far away until I was older.

Then there were five siblings at home.

We never went on holiday, we sometimes visited Grandad in Liverpool,
Sinking our hands in his money jar to see what we could get out was cool.
He was a big man with big hands and Grandma was in hospital with cancer,
Something I didn't understand and I was too young for my parents to answer.

We were stood in the kitchen one day to say bye to Mum and she had suitcases,
Not sure where she was going, was she holidaying alone to nice places?
Not really understanding that my parents had fallen out and feeling very sad,
I never heard them shout and fight, were we were the ones that were bad?

At 9, I wasn't a mummy's boy or a softy but perhaps a sensitive one,
I was crying profusely, it broke my heart, I am her second youngest son.
My sister Linda left 3 weeks later, she had no plans to be a Cinderella,
She was 16, she had planned to leave and soon after to live with her fella.

Then there were four siblings at home.

We saw Mum now and again when we went to dinner at the weekend,
Russ and I took the bus to Rupert Street where she lived just around the bend.
Things weren't too bad I guess and over time we started to understand,
Sometimes meeting her after her work and go to her new home hand in hand.

Dad worked hard, he often left very early for work but Dean was there,
Dean looked after us and made sure we had breakfast and took care.
Off to school, collecting Beverly from the Police House[1] and off we walked,
Passing the children's home and old folks' home and on the way we talked.

School was mostly okay, I thought it was not normal to have dinner tickets,
A single-parent thing which I didn't understand and sneaking extra biscuits.
I encountered my first bully there sadly, Derek from the children's home,
He was jealous I was popular with the other kids and he was always alone.

We didn't do much at the weekends but summer in the 70s were hot,
Across the road from the house watching Dean play footie with his lot.
Dad was off to the betting office and then he was watching the horses,
Dean made us bangers and beans and smash and passed us the sauces.

Not forgetting Uncle Stan, Aunty Milly and our cousins next door,
Milly often came over to help and we went to her if we needed more.
Uncle Arthur lived with us for a time when Dad helped him about,
Well, he lived in the garage until Dad had enough and kicked him out.

Dad loved his maroon Ford Cortina, 1970/71, registration AUA 501J,
I went with him often to the car wash, pretending to drive and play.
He often brought home brand-new lorries to deliver somewhere the next day,
Including chassis with half a cab, I watched him leave and waved him away.

The junior school clique was me, Shaun, the other Neil, Mick and Steve,
John went to Walverden but was in the clique later and Jayne was with me.
Me and Jayne were together from about 8 to 13, a long time and it was great,
We were all destined to go to the same High School so I guess it was fate.

Castercliffe behind us now and off down to Shaffi's in the Arndale market,
To buy high school uniform, including green blazer, Clarks shoes and PT kit.
Walton High School, nice badge on our blazer, very exciting times ahead,
It was fun until we had to learn, "I must concentrate," the teachers said.

Russ and I had good local friends, Ray, up the road and John and Paul too,
Ray was a bit older than us and John and Paul were the same age as us two.
My second bully was another Paul who always picked on Russ and I,
So, I confronted him and asked him for a fight and we had a scrap, do-or-die.

Now and again, we did a sleepover to Linda and Keith at the weekend,
We went camping once, learning to fish, it was windy and it rained no end.
Dad's new girlfriend Thelma moved nearby with her large family,
Three girls; Catherine, Denise and Julie and brothers Tony and Barry.

I got on with Thelma's lot very well, especially the girls anyway,
The girls and I would walk to school and pick up Caroline along the way.
I sometimes walked to school with John but lacking common sense?
Instead of walking the long way round, we would jump over the back fence.

Dean left home after he left his school at Primet[2], it was time to go he says,
He is a good big brother and If I was honest, I would have preferred if he stays.
We didn't see much of him after that but he was nearby out and about,
We sadly learned that he was now leaving town to go down south no doubt.

Then there were three siblings at home.

Peer pressure saw me smoking my first cigarette behind the dining hall,
It wasn't nice, I should have been with the other kids, probably playing football.
The first year went very quick and I was glad the second year did too,
Finishing the first two years was a real blast, the third year comes soon.

I dedicate this last verse to my wife Marion[3], she had it much worse than me,
At only 18 months old, her older brother died in a traffic accident, you see.
They sadly lost their Mama to cancer when Marion was only 9 years old, so sad,
Life at home with just Papa and Frank and without Mama must have been so bad.
I had both parents at 9 and Marion and her brother had just their Papa at home,
Then Frank went to live with Oma and Marion stayed with Papa all alone.
Their Papa died young too when Marion was only 16, now fending for herself,
It is sad our children and I never met her Eltern, their Großeltern ourselves.

---

[1] Beverly's family home was the local Police House and her dad was the local bobby/policeman.
[2] Primet High School, Colne, Lancashire, England.
[3] Marion is a German national.

David, Dad (Yolanda) and Keith at the rear. Russ and me (Neal) at the front.

Me (Neal) and Yolanda approx. 1979.

2. Teenager (Part 2 of 4)

My niece Yolanda was born, I bought her a ladybird book, I was ecstatic,
I saw her first in the family, after Daddy Keith of course, the day was fantastic.
She was born on Saturday 12 August 1978, she was beautiful and so tiny,
Born at 9.37 in the morning and weighed in at 6lb 8oz and her face was so shiny.

Now ask me for the details of my children's births, not got a clue after the date.

So, Dean went to live with relations in Leighton Buzzard down south,
He got a job at Lipton's Tea factory and news home was word of mouth.
It was David's turn to be big brother now but we fended for ourselves,
Back to school to learn (I think), hidden and smoking waiting for the bells.

Unfortunately, us 3 lads were arguing and many times we were grounded,
Like 3 men in 3 separate cells with our bikes and trolleys impounded.
Feeling brave one night, I climbed out of the window and David observed,
He probably thought that when I got caught, I would get what I deserved.

I ran away to the park[1] and Thelma's girls were there in the pavilion,
I told them I escaped and sat with them and they called me a villain.
Dad and Thelma rolled up in the car at the gate and walked up in the dark,
Under the bench behind their legs when they asked if they had seen me in the park.

Some weekends we went to the outdoor swimming pool but had no cash,
We perfected sneaking in and disappearing through the trees in a flash.
Sometimes we would walk around the golf course collecting the lost balls,
And sell them back to the golfers playing there and jump back over the walls.

Well, thirteen to nearly sixteen at Walton High School should be a breeze,
I say after finishing last in something on Sports Day and getting off my knees.
Had I put my mind into it, with lessons and this race, I would have finished first,
I mucked around, flirted and smoked, I never skived but was one of the worst.

Mum moved to Taunton, Somerset then off to join NAAFI[2] in Germany,
She learned German classes at Mülheim an der Ruhr and her life was harmony.
I sadly didn't see her much after that, such is life but I never blamed her,
She had a happy life and if she wanted to see us, she knew where we were.

Learning French with Mr Crew and German with Frau Sauer was frustrating,
I would rather do Geography with Miss Riddiough which was much more exciting.
Religious Education with Mr Wilkinson was something to miss in the main,
Always in trouble, letters home to Dad and 'bend over' for Mr Williams's cane.

What the hell do I need to learn German for? Frau Sauer tried to teach me how,
I remember her saying that I might need it one day, if only she knew me now.
I was part of the popular tough guys with John and Shaun, what went wrong?
I actually enjoyed Music class, being a part of the choir and singing a song.

At about this time there was an intimidating family moved in behind us,
An Irish family; 4 overpowering boys at home but the parents were no fuss.
There were also 2 older brothers who lived nearby and Chris was about my age,
I snubbed his dominance until we crossed paths at 17 but that is another page.

The best thing about being about 13 to 16 was going to Shaun's farm after school,
Dad said it was okay as long as I was home before dark, Shaun's farm was cool.
Shaun's mum would collect us after school and we would drive home to the horses,
Just before dark, I would run home mostly downhill, over walls and the golf courses.

Shaun was tough at school but at home he was always training hard on his horse,
Concentrating and timing how long it takes him to get around the jump course.
He was very good on his horse and won many rosettes in the many competitions,
Travelling all weekend to Park Hall Equestrian Centre, Huntingdon exhibitions.

Shaun's parents Tony and Jean were always good to me and his sisters were too,
Lynn and Carol were alright, Carol was closer, nearly the same age as us two.
Shaun was the junior rider and his Aunty Pat was the semi-retired senior you see,
Cousin Tony was a blacksmith and his dad Peter was wrestler Tally Ho from the TV.
RIP to his parents and also Lynn too who sadly died from COVID.

My sort of job was to help Shaun with his horses, tackle, feeding and mucking out,
It was fun really, having many laughs, smoking and generally just fooling about.
My wage I suppose was hot meals and Shaun would share his cash with me,
Plus, we had our own little earner, selling people sacks of horse manure after tea.

Another job was working on Saturday with my pal John, his mum helped us find it,
Mucking out the stinking, noisy chicken coops was hard, up to our ankles in shit.
Sunday paper round was an early start, going to the newsagent to pick up the bag,
A long walk around the houses and up and down the hills was a necessary drag.

Going to school along the cinder path passed the graveyard to get to the shop,
Down Walton Lane to school and to the blue corner shop to buy sweets and pop.
Getting an adult to buy us cigarettes with the money we probably pocketed or saved,
Jumping the fence into school next to the running track and giving Jayne a wave.

Another friend who deserves a mention was Peter who was a year older than me,
He lived nearby on Rimmington Place with a big garden and a swing in the tree.
His big brother Wayne and big sister Yvonne were nice but much older than us,
Peter's parents were well spoken and his mum was kind and always made a fuss.

Sadly, I didn't get the education guidance at home but only have myself to blame,
Finishing high school was nothing to brag about and not doing well is a shame.
Hindsight is a wonderful thing and I wish I had done better, finishing with nothing,
The aspiration of joining the Navy but the entrance test and medical wasn't promising.

---

[1] Marsden Park Nelson, Lancashire, England.
[2] NAAFI—Navy, Army and Air Force Institutes is a company created by the British government on 9 December 1920 to run recreational establishments needed by the British Armed Forces, and to sell goods to servicemen and women and their families.

Me (Neal) and Nadina approx. 1982.

Yolanda, Wesley and me (Neal) and Nadina approx. 1982.

3. Leaving Home (Part 3 of 4)

So, where did we leave it? From being a middle-aged teenager,
I wasn't even 16 when I left school, about a month earlier if I remember.
David almost 18 and off he went, leaving just Russell and I to it,
Dad always away, a proper big brother to Russell now as I do my bit.

Then there were two siblings at home.

Rather than let Dad give me a hard time for leaving school with nothing,
I will get my bones down to the job centre to find a job and do something.
The person behind the desk was not very sympathetic about my nonsense,
Not answering yes to any of their questions apart from I had a residence.

I am not proud of leaving school with nothing, it is even more alarming now,
My children did very well at school thank God and I probably advised them how.
At this point, in the job centre and looking through the vacancies and daydream,
All those good jobs with a good wage up for grabs and I just wanted to scream.

For the time being, a YTS job (Youth Training Scheme) position was the way,
A 6-month on-the-job training course working for the environment Monday to Friday.
The wages were peanuts but at least Dad understood and as long as I paid board,
So off to this lake at Catlow Bottoms[1], walking or riding a bike and the rain poured.

It was actually interesting, building foot tracks and fishing platforms around the lake,
I was proving an asset and doing a good job getting dimensions right, give or take.
It was a shame that the job was only 6 months but at least it was an entry on my CV,
To the job centre on Monday to see what other jobs or a YTS job they have for me.

YTS, it is then, and again Dad was okay with it as I'm not hanging about like a yob,
No, this man is back on someone's books bringing in the ca$h, I have another job.
This time in Lomeshaye Industrial Estate, Nelson doing some kind of packaging,
A bit boring actually and not as interesting as the other job and needs no thinking.

By the end of each week, I boasted a plaster on each finger from paper-cuts,
You all know how paper-cuts are, they hurt like hell and not funny, this job sucks.
Nevertheless, I carried on, packing gifts, cards and stuff into a box and sealed it,
The little brown envelope with my very small wages in my pocket but I won't quit.

£25 a week was not much, another YTS under my belt and another entry on the CV,
Back at the job centre and feeling a bit more confident with myself, I see a vacancy.
ASDA's new bakery needed an unqualified labourer and off to the interview I go,
The wages were not bad, they were happy with me and my CV and I couldn't say no.

I start at what time on Monday morning? 4 am, that's the witching hour by the way,
So, Sunday after some form of scoff, I tucked myself in to be ready for my first day.
It's still flipping dark for starters and toddling off to Colne, well the border anyway,
The bright-lit car park (what a waste of money) and where do I go? By the way.

Finding my way in and still in time (obviously) and smelling my way to work,
Fresh bread smells good and 2 bosses were there and like me dressed like a twerp.
Dressed all in white and they wore white cowboy hats and mine was more of a net,
So many machines, mixing heavy dough and scoffing jam donuts, is my life set?

Starting at 4 am and finishing at 12, 1 or 2 was not fair and it was hard to complain,
Being late now and again and off to the Human Resources (HR) office was a pain.
The only good thing about the job was taking surplus jam donuts for Thelma's lot,
Back to HR and they asked me to leave or be sacked which left me in a bit of a spot.

Signed on the dole and eventually got my first Giro and back looking for a job,
Two medical incidents followed, a broken nose because I flirted with a girl of a yob.
Finally giving in to my bunion and another operation and donning a plaster cast,
On crutches, hanging out in the Arndale[2] feeling sorry for myself and hope it won't last.

In the Arndale, on the balcony and unexpectedly saw my bro Dean coming in,
I shouted to him and he acknowledged and waved and I hobbled down to him.
It must have looked funny (for him at least) seeing his little brother on crutches,
He did his Dean look, laughed and from that day forward, he calls me Peggers.

Dad not impressed and we had some kind of fall out which was not usual for us,
He told me to leave home and Thelma stepped in and asked what was all the fuss?
Packing my 2 dustbin bags in my room and then Thelma came upstairs for a talk,
She told me that all I had to do was to apologise to Dad but I decided to walk.

Then there was one sibling at home.

---

[1] The hamlet of Catlow lies 1 mile to the east of Nelson town-centre in Pendle, Lancashire, England. It is a place of historical importance locally but, further back into pre-history, it became archaeologically more important for its Middle Bronze-Age burial sites, which were sadly destroyed in the mid-19th Century.

[2] Arndale (Shopping Centre) downtown Nelson, Lancashire, England.

4. Finding MY Way (Part 4 of 4)

I stayed at a girlfriend's house, but no one was happy that I lived in their abode,
I then moved into a room at her Uncle Paul and Aunt Carol's house, up the road.
When the girlfriend and I split, luckily Paul and Carol said I could stay at theirs,
Paul chatted about his proud time in the army which he had done in previous years.

My new girlfriend (of the same name) was visiting and Chris knocked on the door,
"Do you remember Chris readers?" The dominating geezer from a few years before.
Chris was now with my ex and he threatened me, that I was seeing her again,
Paul told him I was not with his niece; and my new girlfriend had the same name.

Now 18 and legally allowed to frequent Nelson's finest so off to the Station[1],
Meeting up with Shaun and drinking a few and then off to the Lord Nelson[2].
Saturday nights were great, clubbing at the Sands[3] under the Arndale,
I saw my bro David and his girlfriend Carol dancing, drinking shorts and ale.

Life was not brilliant and needed change so I left Nelson for pastures new,
I moved to Burnley and moved in with a girl initially for a month or two.
She was pregnant from another and my family was against my decision,
Always confrontation, moving and after the baby was born, there was division.

We decided to call it a day with regards to the relationship and I left them to it,
It was sad for her baby as he was so young and I also left my Angora rabbit.
I moved to not that far away, to a house across from Prestige into a bedsit,
I didn't see them again until I needed a form signing for something and that's it.

I was quite happy in my bedsit, my own space, no stress and listening to music,
Christopher Cross singing *Ride Like the Wind* on my record player, slick.
This is where I met Gary, a top bloke and it is a shame there is now no contact,
He was a bit of a smoothie and a good wingman with the girls and all that.

Another couple of good mates from the Trafalgar Flats were Mick and Woz,
Dossing in Towneley Park after magic mushrooms, hallucinating and seeing stars.
Why did I did I try this? I tried it once and not again thank you very much,
Still good blokes though, good times and a shame we didn't stay in touch.

It was safer enjoying Gary's company and playing pool at Playland,
We were both bragging Pool Kings but after a zillion games it got bland.
This is where I met the next girlfriend and she could even play pool,
I would nip out of Playland to go and meet her from her school.

Not something I would readily admit but she was only 4 years younger,
In her final year of high school and her family were cool and I liked her.
She was the first girl I took home to visit family but I lied about her age,
I was not embarrassed but did not want a hard time at this stage.

Her family were Burnley fans, "come on you Clarets," they would shout,
It was not serious and it was an 'on and off' when we were out and about.
Dean was courting with Linda, I saw Dad now and again and my sister,
Linda had 4 kids now; Yolanda, Wesley, Nadina and Ashley the baby brother.

Feeling a bit useless, unemployed and not really focussed so I had to decide,
Losing pool against Gary and off to Burnley Army Careers Office and applied.
Nervously visiting an ex to get a form signed that I had no responsibilities etc.
My family thought I was joking that I was off and that I was a bit of a waffler.

When I came back after the first 4 weeks, they were all so proud of me,
They didn't expect me to get that far, something for me to prove in the army.
The on-off girlfriend was still on-off and eventually I asked her ultimately,
Was she interested in coming with me to Germany? and the rest is history.

Girlfriend's names intentionally omitted.

---

[1] Station Hotel/Bar, Nelson, Lancashire, England.
[2] The Lord Nelson Pub, Nelson, Lancashire, England.
[3] The Sands Nightclub, Nelson, Lancashire, England.

5. Boot Camp

All the players at Turf Moor were English apart from Phil Harrington,
I was standing on the Longside thinking I'd had enough, I was done.
Just before Christmas 1984 with my mates playing pool at Playland,
Life was not good, unemployed at the time and thinking all this is bland.
Playing against Gary and I said if I lost the game, I was going to join the army,
Obviously, Gary and the others watching said 'bullshit' and that I was 'barmy.'

From one thought to the other, not even discussing it with family, off I went,
Walking to Burnley Army Careers Office to swap my bedsit for an army tent.
After the chat, I passed the 'Entrance Test' and I asked "where do I sign?"
I had to read the 'Oath of Allegiance' out loud, sign it and the job was mine.
They gave me joining instructions, a travel warrant to camp and some cash,
Enlisted, and starting in January, so short back and sides and trim my tash.

On the bus to Skipton and then Nick got on the bus in Nelson,
A school pal of my younger brother and he was already in training, well done.
We talked about nothing but the army and our futures, he was a great lad,
Going forward in time out of respect, Nick sadly died when he was only 42, so sad.
I will never forget him and the help he gave me in training, I was not alone,
Friends to the end and I helped his best friend Ron pay for a nice gravestone.
Rest in peace, my friend.

Arrival was scary, everyone shouting, getting a haircut but I'd already had it,
So, I whined to the soldier that I had already had a cut and he said "it was shit."
Not leaving it there, the soldier told the barber to "take off his stupid tash too,"
QM's (Quartermasters) for kit and the "KFS (knife, fork and spoon) are for you."
Up at the crack of dawn, snow on the ground, standing in a group and freezing,
Dressed in green coveralls, then sort of marching to breakfast and sniffling.

How can you eat it in 5 minutes? as soon as I sat down it was time to go,
Back to our room for a welcome brief and then learn to iron and sew.
Not sure why I need to learn this, ha-ha, and buying many cans of starch,

Ironing denims, KF shirts, jumpers and bulling our boots ready for the march.
It was funny watching the men all around me, arms and legs all over the place,
Left, right, left, right, walking and not properly marching, we were a disgrace.

Our first four weeks are going to be hell before we Pass Off the Square,
Berets and cap badges and first leave home was far off, I can do this, I swear.
Waterloo Platoon, not knowing military history and not sure what it all means,
We need to learn regimental history and what battle honours are, it seems.
Our section commander, Corporal (Cpl) 'Mick' shouted, "outside, photo time is here,"
Me, Smudge, Bako and Baz at the front and Galla, Scouse, Plummy and H at the rear.

The Battle of Waterloo[1] was fought on Sunday 18th June 1815, 210 years ago,
A French army under the command of Napoleon was defeated you know.
This battle honour is a proud honour and a very important day for me now,
My future regiment, the Queen's Lancashire Regiment will show me how.
Already feeling proud and now craving to overcome this first four weeks,
Learning drill; how to properly march and salute and other drill techniques.

Passing Off the Square and awarded our berets and cap badges was a good day,
My family were not there though and then journeying home with 4-weeks' pay.
Not allowed to wear uniform on leave was unfair so I had no idea why I took it,
Changing into uniform on the train and disobeying direct orders seemed to fit.
Family teased me a little, wondering if I can hack the training and the rest of it,
I really can do this; "back to barracks now people so I will see you in a bit."

Indoor PT first thing; white t-shirt, blue shorts and plimsoles on parade,
5-minute scoff, followed by PT with Corporal 'Mal,' vomiting and requiring aid.
Learning the core values such as courage, discipline and integrity,
Respect for others, loyalty, selfless commitment and no self-pity.
I hated milling with Glen, it was tough as I dodged most of his blows,
"Did he really win?" I asked, "well you have the bloody-nose so who knows."

Battle PT with red t-shirts, denims and boots and march to the gym,
BFT (Basic Fitness Test) was hard, and the chance to pass it was slim.
Battle PT included doing a CFT (Combat Fitness Test), another hard test,
CFT is a 2-hour march with helmet, webbing[2], weight and weapons, and no rest.
Running and assault course in squads, teamwork and carrying logs,
Cold, wet and covered in shit and pissed off and often stuck in bogs.

Four months to push before we have our Passing Out Parade in Best Dress,
Every day, learning new things, getting fit and running through mud is a mess.
Change-Parades were crap, in this uniform and back on and off with changes,
Back out in combat dress, with webbing, helmet and rifle ready for the ranges.
Fieldcraft was next on the programme; stealthily crawling through more mud,
Camouflaged up to the hilt, trying to hide until you were observed by Big Jud.

I remember one day when I was on guard duty and guarding the gate,
A military coach arrived and I let it through, and then I heard "hello mate."
That was a familiar voice and I turned around and it was my big bro,
He was a high-ranking soldier and this coach was his people you know.
Steve was a Bandmaster[3] and his regimental band were on a tour,
Invited to the Sergeants' Mess; it was such an insight and much more.

I embarrassingly got into trouble for pinching someone's army jumper,
My award; RP's (Restriction of Privileges) and to clean floors with the bumper.
I wasn't the best soldier and often found myself on Show Parade at Ten,
First in Best Dress and then into PT Kit and then other kit, again and again.
I questioned myself, "is this really for me?" and something had to give,
I was one of the best runners and best shots, I had myself to forgive.

Cleaning weapons[4] was a necessary chore and there were so many parts,
Dismantling them and then reassemble on the clock with many restarts.
Then do it again in the dark; SLR, GPMG, SMG and Pistol to name a few,
Also; two-inch mortar, LAW 80, grenades and load/unload magazines too.
First aid; 4B's; Breathing, Bleeding, Burns and 'broken' Bones, priority importance,
Learn 5P's next; Planning and Preparation beats a Piss Poor Performance.

(It is 7P's today)[5]

Then came the Depot SAAM (Skill At Arms Meeting) Shooting Competition,
I needed a miracle if I was to proceed to Germany, a winner's position.
I was on Commanding Officer's (CO's) interviews and he gave congratulations,
He told me that overall, I had earned the right for the Pass Out celebrations.
Again, no family to see my Passing Out Parade, nevertheless a proud day,
Sergeant (Sgt) 'Smudge' invited me to sit with his family for lunch so it worked out okay.

Next up, after leave and off to Luton Airport for my flight to Germany…

A little history; the King's Division, formed in 1968 (with the union of the Lancastrian, Yorkshire and North Irish Brigades) is a British army command, training and administrative apparatus designated for infantry regiments in the north of England. The Depot was established at Queen Elizabeth Barracks in Strensall near York. The division changed over time with reorganisation and amalgamations. At the time of my training, the regiments are below (which also includes the duration of their existence in the division and various brigades):

The King's Own Royal Border Regiment (1959–2006)
The King's Regiment (1958–2006)
The Prince of Wales's Own Regiment of Yorkshire (1958–2006)
The Green Howards (Alexandra, Princess of Wales's Own Regiment of Yorkshire) (1688–2006)
The Duke of Wellington's Regiment (West Riding) (1881–2006)
The Queen's Lancashire Regiment[6] (1970–2006)
Thank you to Waterloo Platoon, the King's Division instructors.

Lieutenant (Lt) 'Sir'	The Green Howards (Alexandra, Princess of Wales's Own Regiment of Yorkshire)
Sgt 'Smudge'	The King's Own Royal Border Regiment
Cpl 'Carlisle'	The Prince of Wales's Own Regiment of Yorkshire
Cpl 'Jud'	The Duke of Wellington's Regiment (West Riding)
Cpl 'Spike'	The Green Howards (Alexandra, Princess of Wales's Own Regiment of Yorkshire)
Cpl 'Mick'	The King's Regiment
Cpl 'Mal'(PTI)	The King's Regiment

PTI (Physical Training Instructor)

---

[1] Battle of Waterloo—I visited the location in Belgium (in 1815 the location was the United Kingdom of the Netherlands, now in Belgium).
[2] Webbing—Personal Load Carrying Equipment (PLCE) is the current tactical webbing system of the British army. The webbing consists of a belt, yoke (shoulder harness) and a number of pouches to carry things you need for battle, a significant weight.

[3] Bandmaster (Appointment)—Warrant Officer Class One (same as a Regimental Sergeant Major (Appointment)) the highest rank before becoming a Commissioned Officer. Other (Non-Commissioned Officer) army ranks in order are; Private (me), Lance Corporal, Corporal, Sergeant, Colour/Staff Seargeant, Warrant Officer Class Two (the rank I held on retirement) (a Company Sergeant Major for example). Commissioned Officer Ranks; 2nd Lieutenant, Lieutenant, Captain, Major, Lieutenant Colonel, Colonel, Brigadier, Major General, Lieutenant General and General. A Field Marshal is currently an honorary rank.

[4] SLR-L1A1 Self-Loading Rifle 7.62mm, GPMG-L7A2 General-Purpose Machine-Gun belt-fed 7.62mm, SMG—Sterling Sub-Machine Gun 9mm, Pistol—Browning Hi-power 9mm, Two-inch mortar—crew (2) 51mm approx. 8 rounds a minute, LAW 80—Light Anti-armour Weapon 80 94mm rocket-propelled grenade. Grenades—Mills bomb. There are more weapons to learn/use once you get to your battalion.

[5] 7P's—Proper Planning and Preparation Prevents Piss Poor Performance.

[6] My Regiment from training until I transferred to the Adjutant General's Corps (Staff and Personnel Support) in 1994.

Army training day one (Jan-May 1985), Strensall, York. Rear Galla, Scouse, Plummy, and H. Front me (Neal), Smudge, Bako, Baz and Jim.

Waterloo Platoon Passing Out Parade May 1985.

6. Deutschland
(German, Germany in English)

Army training complete, time with family and off to Luton and there were no tears,
I flew to Germany late spring 1985 where I was to be stationed for a few years.
My first time on an aircraft and the first time abroad as I am off to my promised land,
My first reaction was the warmer weather compared to home in the north of England.
I think back to school and wished I paid more attention at German with Frau Sauer,
She was good to me; she was very patient with everyone and I did respect her.

Here I am, my new home for a few years in Paderborn, a city in western Germany,
My first impression was that the city was very clean, there was no litter, it was so tidy.
The Romanesque Dom[1] in the city centre has been standing since the 13th century,
Paderborn has the shortest river in Germany, the Pader, also known as the Spree.
I know I am going to like it here; I love the city and of course the alluring nightlife,
Little did I know that my first was to be born here as this is where I meet my wife.

My only sad time being in Germany was when I was homesick at the beginning,
I would get the Transline[2] coach across Europe home to family time and partying.
If I am honest, the other sad times were when we went on manoeuvres and how,
The local ranges and training areas and also the cattle train[3] to cold, rainy Soltau[4].
The German food was good though, especially the bratties when you were cold,
Wolfgang drove from Sennelager[5] to Soltau with his 'schnelli wagon[6]' truth be told.

I learn more about Paderborn when I courted my wife who was born in the vicinity,
Marion was born in Salzkotten[7], she called her birthplace jokingly Salt Lake City.
Actually, a town in the district of Paderborn which was famous for its salt production,
Meeting her family who were scattered in neighbouring villages was an introduction.
The small attractive villages were my first-hand sample of how Germans were living,
Here we are, my new wife and new daughter Vanessa with relatives who are loving.

The elderly clean the paths and curbs outside their homes like their lives depend,
The cold seasonal weather does not stop these old folk pick up leaves without end.
Having lived in Germany for over half of my life, I can say that I have no misgivings,

The majority of the houses are different in sizes, shapes, colours and trimmings.
So, what else has this historical divided[8] country got to offer me over my future time?
Watching Germany transpire as the fruitions of East and West reunify was sublime.

The first time I was stationed in Berlin was at the very end of the Cold War[9],
The centre of West Berlin was ore inspiring and free, East Berlin was still quite poor.
Thankfully, for me, this division of sorts was transitioning before my very eyes,
You could say that West Berlin stood still as East Berlin was beginning to rise.
The second time I was stationed in Berlin was a decade later and it amazed me,
The *real* centre of the now one city beckoning its history in this now thriving city.

After a second short stint in the UK[10], my next stop in Germany was Münster,
Historically like Paderborn and here we were blessed with our daughter Hannah.
I was based mainly in North Rhine-Westphalia, a western German state,
I was also based in Bergen-Hohne in a northern state, with sadly much debate.
Bergen-Belsen on Anne-Frank-Platz lies just down the road where birds don't fly,
The former POW[11], concentration and displaced persons camp where visitor's cry.

The next city I moved to was Gütersloh famous for cabaret to theatre to jazz,
Next was Köln, famous for its Christmas market and carnivals with razzmatazz.
Köln has the most famous cathedral in Germany and is near to Phantasialand,
Just one of the theme parks that we still visit to this day which is grand.
Other places of interest throughout our lives included Ketteler Hof and Movie Park,
Belantis in Leipzig, Zoos in Berlin and Köln, and Safari Land in Stukenbrock.

Holidaying with Mum in a residential park near Winterberg in Hochsauerland[12],
Also, day-tripping with Mum to the famous 'Dambusters,' Möhnesee Dam.
Overnighting in Lübeck famous for marzipan, and Heidelburg enroute to Italy,
Heide Park and even Colditz Castle, seemingly one extreme to another, literally.
My liaison and embassy work took me alone; north, east, south and west,
Hamburg, Hammelburg, Koblenz and München but Idar-Oberstine[13] was best.

JHQ[14] near Mönchengladbach was my final station before I retired from the army,
An enclosed secure place, an exclusive military town with absolutely every amenity.
The Mosel River Region, Trier to Koblenz and return by cycle was a highlight,
All the picturesque towns and villages along the river are an unforgettable sight.
I retire here and stay in Germany and move nearby to our home today in Erkelenz,
Near to the Dutch border and famous for its 'Electrisize Festival,' a new commence.

Autobahns (motorways) are vast and are not claustrophobic as they are in the UK, As the Germans light-heartedly say, "on the island" at the cliffs, there is no escape.

It is law to be roadworthy on your bicycle and having a bell gives you clear passage, Ring-ring your bell and people (and with dogs) move which is such an advantage. But equally if you do not have a bell you might have to slow down to stop to pass, Mopeds/scooters (50cc) are allowed on most of *Holland's* designated bike paths.

---

[1] Dom—German for Cathedral.

[2] Transline—English/German Bus Company, primarily used by British army personnel and their families transporting them from/to UK and Germany.

[3] Cattle train—a metaphor, the train would move on the rails, not at peak times and with many stops, sort of overnight like cattle and freight and taking eons for perhaps a normally short journey.

[4] Soltau is a mid-sized town in the Lüneburg Heath in the district of Heidekreis, in Lower Saxony. Military training areas.

[5] Sennelager is a village that forms part of the City of Paderborn. The military ranges and training areas.

[6] Schnelli wagon—German for fast-food vehicle.

[7] Salzkotten (in English, "Salt cottages").

[8] At the Potsdam Conference (17 July to 2 August 1945), after Germany's unconditional surrender on 8 May 1945, the Allies officially divided Germany into the four military occupation zones—France in the southwest, the United Kingdom in the northwest, the United States in the south, and the Soviet Union in the east. East and West Germany. Then came the Cold War until the fall of the Berlin Wall on 9 November 1989. Soviet-occupied East Germany, officially known as the German Democratic Republic, was reunited with West Germany on 3 October 1990.

[9] The Cold War officially was from 12 March 1947 until Christmas Day 1991. Berlin was at the forefront of the Cold War when it was sadly divided, East; the Soviet Sector and the West, Allies; French, British and the USA. The Wall was erected on 13 August 1961. The falling of the Berlin Wall was 9 November 1989.

[10] UK—Gave us our middle child, our son Matthew was born in York.

[11] POW—Prisoners of War, this camp was liberated on 15 April 1945 by the British 11th Armoured Division. The soldiers discovered approximately 60,000 prisoners inside, most of them half-starved and seriously ill, and another 13,000 corpses lying around the camp unburied. A memorial with an exhibition hall currently stands at the site. I also visited a Nazi concentration camp at Sachsenhausen, Oranienburg. One of the first detention facilities established by the Nazis in the state of Prussia when they gained power in 1933. It lies north of Berlin.

[12] This park is now owned/run by Centre Parcs. (it is spelled 're' in Ge/Ne).

[13] Idar-Oberstine was where Bruce Willis was born.

[14] JHQ—Joint Headquarters near Mönchengladbach.

Beginning of military career—Jim, Glen and Neal, Paderborn 1986. (Germany)

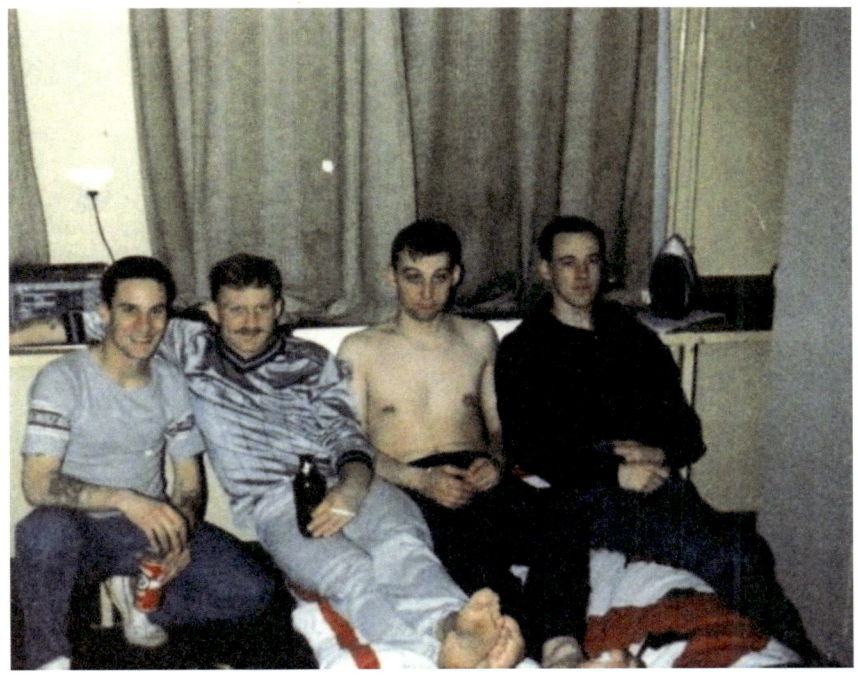

Beginning of military career—Glen, Neal, Jim and Rob, Paderborn 1987. (Germany)

End of military career (Germany)—Neal and Marion last Mess event 2011.

End of military career (Germany)—Neal 2011.

7. Canucks

Joining my regiment in Paderborn, Germany in June 1985, a long time ago,
I was not there for 2 months; before tolerating my last bully so morale was low.
We naturally say that bullying doesn't happen in the army, that's just too far,
Off to the airport with a marked face to fly to Canada on a Royal Air Force Tristar.

Flying to Canada, refuelling in Reykjavik, Iceland then onwards to Calgary,
No smoking is hard, everyone talking about the temperature on the prairie.
The flight seemed to take a whole day to get there, but not losing a day,
Losing a day flying back though, the pads[1] "can't wait for then," they say.

Loaded on the coaches to Camp Crowfoot, Suffield, Alberta, some 250 km,
This particular trip was my longest time in Canada, about 8 weeks in theatre[2].
My shortest time in Canada was literally a long weekend and back to Berlin,
Returning home on compassionate grounds, feeling for my wife from within.

I have experienced Exercise MEDICINE MAN[3] several times and it is hard,
Infantry soldier most times and by far the hardest which even left me scarred.
Attached to Engineers[4] was much easier, working in a command vehicle,
Implementing engineer support which in a war footing concept is critical.

Numerous exercises per year here, extremely low to high temperatures,
A very dusty prairie where you can count the trees but not the creatures.
This poem culminates all my times in Canada but primarily the first one,
Infantryman on exercise, then R&R[5] and then adventure training was fun.

Climatising for a few days first thank God, getting used to the time and heat,
A couple of km walk to Ralston and our first taste of the CANEX[6] street.
Everything in the shop is either military stuff or First Nations[7] memorabilia,
Before long we were off down to the dustbowl[8] to deploy on to the area.

Attacking was hard, debussing from our APC's[9] carrying the varied weapons,
Live-firing[10] training, war-like and having to debus[11] and take defence in seconds.
Then pepper potting[12] and skirmishing[13] through the dust and sweating profusely,
Hiding in a defence position a while and to cool down, we undo our jackets loosely.

Digging holes in the harsh hard dusty prairie ground was really hard graft[14],
Mostly wearing our Mark IV metal helmets[15] deep in the trench with no draught.
Accidentally[16] hit by a pick axe flat blade in the back hurt like hell which left a scar,
Then casevacked[17] to the med centre by helicopter for assessment seemed far.

Trench warfare in the 80s is no small feat which takes our training further,
The best defence is a good offence because you can hold out much longer.
I remember telling Oma[18] the 'trench scar' was when I was shot, a silly joke,
I then told her I was kidding, the girlfriend called me an idiot, I am *butt* a bloke.

Night time was silent and it would be extremely dark without the northern lights,
The beautiful dancing waves of light which captivates us, what a remarkable sight.
The silence and darkness do not stay that way for long, as we are at war after all,
A para illum[19] glows the sky and a thunder flash[20] is heard and "stand to"[21] is called.

Attacking in the direction of the dustbowl was hard as our sweat poured,
Seemingly, doing this over and over for weeks and 'EndEx'[22] is finally called.
The first real shower in weeks and a cold Labatt Blue beer is the priority,
R&R time sees us driving to Lethbridge and the illustrious Medicine Hat City.

The Trans-Canada Highway to 'The Hat,' the bars were full of friendly folks,
"They were all wearing cowboy hats and dancing!" The good ole Canucks[23].
Drinking pitchers[24] of the varied beers[25] and 'shit kicking[26]' the night away,
Overnighting downtown in the Sin Bin[27] and start all over again the next day.

Medicine Hat beer time and the favourite bar is the Silver Buckle Sports Bar,
The sunniest city in Canada and the Canucks driving extravagant long cars.
Woolworths here is the biggest supermarket in the world as far as I am concerned,
Buying Michael Jackson, Paul Young and Wham cassette tapes with money earned.

This time R&R here and Lethbridge, in the future Calgary in a hired 80s Ford,
Column gear shifter and 3 seat bench front and rear is what we can afford.
Our regimental brother; Derek was tragically killed in an RTA in the US,
RIP Derek, a sad time for the boys, a formidable footballer had sadly left us.

As the newbie, I was nominated to stay behind for adventure training,
Sort of knowing what it entailed and really looking forward to the cycling.
So off up-country to both Jasper and Banff National Parks, many miles,
Kayaking Banff's mountain lakes and rivers and hiking many trails.

The Plain of Six Glaciers trail which surrounds Lake Louise is impressive,
I am here for free and know this expedition would be extremely expensive.
Cycling next; from Lake Louise and mostly downhill to Radium Hot Springs,
A perfect place to rest those weary muscles, it is just one of them things.

Jasper next and staying at the Lucerne Campground is on the cards,
A camp fire with new friends and drinking beer and staring at the stars.
Jasper, the largest national park in the Canadian Rockies is breathtaking,
More of the same gladly and abundant views through the Rockies trekking.

So, in a way, the best time in Canada was my first time, this time was amazing,
Back to Calgary for the flight home to Germany and not sure what I am facing.
British Army Training Unit Suffield (BATUS) is still going strong after many years,
From 1971 to present day and the prairie has seen many frontiers and pioneers.

---

[1] Pads—British military slang for married accompanied personnel.
[2] Theatre—In warfare (we are in Canada for warfare live-firing exercise/training) a theatre is an area in which important military events occur or are in progress.
[3] Exercise MEDICINE MAN is the name of the exercise that British army partake in live-firing (armoured and infantry level) at the British Army Training Unit Suffield (BATUS). BATUS is the British army's largest armoured training facility. It is approximately 2,700 square kilometres and the exercise battlegroup is approximately 1400 soldiers.
[4] Engineers—Deployed to Canada with both Royal Electrical and Mechanical Engineers (REME) (Light Aid Detachment (LAD)) and Royal Engineers (Armoured).
[5] R&R—Rest and Recuperation.
[6] CANEX—CANEX has been Canada's Military Store serving the Canadian Armed Forces (CAF) (and British army in this case) with retail operations since 1968.
[7] First Nations—Indigenous peoples in Canada, comprising First Nations, Inuit and Métis. Although Indian or Native is a term still commonly used in Legal issues etc.
[8] Dustbowl—Is the aptly named area at Camp Crowfoot where we met-up with our exercise vehicles. In this case, the finishing line.
[9] APC—Armoured Personnel Carrier, in this case Fighting Vehicle (FV)432.
[10] Live-firing—Live ammunition etc.
[11] Debus—British military slang for alighting from a motor vehicle/unload (personnel or stores) from a vehicle.
[12] Pepper potting—Is a military manoeuvre used when advancing towards the enemy.
[13] Skirmishing—An episode of irregular or unpremeditated fighting, especially between

small or outlying parts of armies.

[14] Graft—Slang for working hard.

[15] Mk IV metal helmet—Is a combat helmet that was used by the British army in the 1950s to 1980s. It was replaced by the composite material Mk 6 helmet in 1985. We received the Mk 6 helmet after this exercise.

[16] Accident—I am with my Company on my first Med Man 'B Company.' The following year was with C Company, that is when I had this accident.

[17] Casevac—Abbreviation for Casualty Evacuation.

[18] Oma—My girlfriend's (at the time; now my wife, Marion's) grandmother.

[19] Para Illum—Battlefield illumination is technology that improves visibility for military forces operating in difficult low-light conditions.

[20] Thunderflash—Used as a training replacement for grenades.

[21] Stand-to—A military alert where all troops are to have weapons ready for action.

[22] EndEx—Is a military term that means 'end of exercise,' and is used to signal when an activity or training has come to a close.

[23] Canucks—A slang name for a Canadian.

[24] Pitcher—A standard sized pitcher holds two litres.

[25] Canadian Beers—Include Molson, Molson Canadian, Molson Export and Molson Coors and Labatt and Labatt Blue to name a few.

[26] Shit kicking—Slang for dancing in Canada. Correct terms are 'Red River Jig,' 'Rabbit Dance,' 'Broom Dance' and 'Sash Dance.' A combination of First Nations dancing and Scottish and French-Canadian step-dancing.

[27] Assiniboia Inn (Sin Bin) in Medicine Hat, Alberta—unfortunately now closed.

Neal (Camp Crowfoot) BATUS, Canada 1985.

Neal adventure training 1 Banff and Jasper, Canada 1985.

Neal adventure training 2 Banff and Jasper, Canada 1985.

John and Neal, (Prairie) BATUS, Canada 1986.

Excerpts of the next poem were first written in 1987 and are primarily my perspective and memories. Some of the detail is extracted from old regimental magazines. The details however, are true and an accurate account to the best of my knowledge. I use slang for religious groups for dramatization effect for the poem and do not mean to sound derogatory. The British military left Northern Ireland (NI) in 2007 and I believe the contents herein hold the security classification of 'unclassified.' Full names are intentionally omitted to rightfully protect identities.

8. Slipper City

We have to begin this poem with a related ill-fated tragedy of 6th March 1987,
MS Herald of Free Enterprise ferry capsized and 193 souls went to heaven.
Most of us were heading for this very crossing, the Zeebrugge ferry disaster,
We were delayed leaving camp for a briefing from our brigade commander.
We missed this journey home where our regiment sadly lost 2; a chef and a wife,
On the dark dock hearing distress from the ship and grateful I didn't lose my life.
Driving to Dunkirk to catch the next ferry when we all should have phoned home,
Cops knocked on my dad's door to confirm my whereabouts, he wasn't alone.

Back from our deserved pre-deployment leave and grateful we missed that ferry,
Continuing with a bit of down time prior to our NI tour and generally being merry.
The night before deployment, talking amongst ourselves and drinking a can or two,
Time to go to Belfast, bye Germany and not sure what we are letting ourselves into.
The Lancashire lads are on the way to Ulster, that troubled place across the bay,
The training in Tin City[1] now behind us, we will probably never forget this day.

My company (B) was based in Girdwood Park co-situated with the Crumlin Road Nick[2],
North Howard Street Mill is one mile to the south where Tac[3] HQ gives SITREPS[4] quick.
The mill, a stone's throw from the Divis Flats also housed the C Company guys,
Fort Whiterock is two miles south west of the mill, that's where A Company lies.
We all had TAOR's[5], areas of responsibility, hard-faced districts of Belfast,
We cannot do this alone; no regiment can work without support that lasts.
'Slipper City' a nickname for Echelon[6]; our admin and supply chain which is crucial,
Situated in the grounds of Musgrave Park Hospital and understandably useful.

We were not there for five minutes before we were briefed for our first patrol,
Getting out there on the streets and back safely is the objective, the goal.
Stop, stop, stop and from the Pigs[7] we debussed[8] quickly to cover, this is for real,
My eyes and barrel of my faithful SLR[9] pointing vigorously and for the trigger I feel.
The early days were the worst, finding our feet and nervously exiting base quick,
Callsign Yankee 24 Charlie[10] is patrolling the busy streets cautiously in our brick[11].
I was tail-end Charlie[12] and found myself alone and surrounded by unruly kids,
A little fearful, shouting for the guys to return and a nearby banger[13] skids.

Back in base, another briefing and never a rest, always on the go,
Remembering that banner on the town hall stating 'Ulster Says No.'
There is always trouble in the province and violence on the street,
In the Ardoyne the Catholics and Protestants were mixing in the heat.
Back on patrol and my turn to wear the bomb-jamming listening device,
Listening intently as it jams signals from the bomber once, twice or thrice.
It is critical but the downfall is that because of something I heard,
I had to stay there with bomb disposal and not like the rest of my herd.

Deployed with the lads and standing guarding a dreaded cordon again,
It was short-lived fame seeing yourself on the TV on News at Ten.
The RUC[14] are always there first and their Hotspurs[15] littering the street,
For those who don't know, the police here are not like a bobby on the beat.
Another riot, give the cops a break, it is all in a day's work for us?
It is over now and the Fire Brigade extinguish flames on a hijacked bus.
Another mobile patrol, top cover[16], VCP's[17] and 'P'[18] checking big-time-players[19],
Sunday church patrol and looking after all religions saying their prayers.

Murals all over the Loyalist houses in Tiger's Bay, red, white and blue,
Fenian's calling us "Brit bastards," we returned-fire with "love you too."
About halfway through the tour was our 5-day R&R[20], a flight home can't be bad,
A flight to Blackpool and onwards to a sports bar in Manchester to meet Dean and Dad.
And, when a typical car backfires, I dive for cover somewhere protected,
And hoping that I don't react to every common bang, something unexpected.
UVF and UDA versus PIRA and INLA[21] are armies that will never rest,
They have been fighting since the sixteenth century to see who is best.

We get more hassle from the Taig's[22] but Prods[23] are sometimes just as bad,
Although I am a British soldier on their land, I think it is horrifying and sad.
Alpha-Whiskey[24] was the novelty of the day, getting a lift to climb high,
Running low on the footie ground and boarding the chopper to fly the sky.
Sangar duty was also one of the jobs, discretely 'P' checking mostly cars,
A fortified tower where we relayed strategic information to Tac HQ from afar.
The high-rise observation post at Templar House in the New Lodge neighbourhood,
Monitoring with high-tech cameras and night vision, which locals never understood.

Iain was killed when he was mobile patrolling the notorious Divis Flats complex,
Terrorists dropped an explosive device on his vehicle, he had high prospects.
Joe was killed when his vehicle was escorting another vehicle to the local police,
Terrorists ambushed his vehicle on Shaw's Road with a burst of automatic fire, RIP.
Belfast took its toll and many other seriously injured casualties were sadly endured,
Slayed cops, Smiler in intensive care for 10 weeks when his loss of leg occurred.
My good pal Casper was hurt by the bomb that killed Iain, it was just devastating,
Ben and Sedge were shot, so many casualties in such a short time was distressing.

I was sadly volunteered to stay behind when my brick went home,
I was part of the handover/takeover teams but was not alone.
Our last day in Northern Ireland is just as important as the first,
Alpha-Whiskey providing our top cover above and I am dying of thirst.
We know it is hot but we have to stay switched on as it is not only our life,
It is up to all of us now and tomorrow we will see our families and good wife.

Epilogue—I do not blame anyone in Northern Ireland who did not want the British army on their land. I was just doing my job. Time really does heal. The Endnote references are at the end of the poem.

---

[1] Tin City—This was a FIBUA (fighting in built up areas) training location in Sennelager, Germany.
[2] Nick—Slang for prison.
[3] Tac—Pronounced TACK, Tactical (Headquarters).
[4] SITREPS—Situation Reports (British military term).
[5] TAOR—Tactical Area of Operational Responsibility.
[6] Echelon—A military company/body of troops providing military support.
[7] Pigs—The Humber Pig was a heavily-armoured truck used by the British army from the mid-1950s until the 1990s.
[8] Debus—British military slang for alighting from a motor vehicle/unload (personnel or stores) from a vehicle.
[9] SLR—The L1A1 Self-Loading Rifle 7.62mm.
[10] Callsign (C/S) Y24C—Predominantly Steve (& Driver), Dougie (Brick Commander), Keith and me.
[11] Brick—An army patrol team of normally 4; point (person at the front), 2 in the middle and tail-end Charlie.
[12] Tail-end Charlie—A person or thing that brings up the rear in a group or formation.
[13] Banger—In this case, a motor vehicle/car.
[14] RUC—Royal Ulster Constabulary.
[15] Hotspurs—The RUC Land Rover Tangi armoured vehicle.
[16] Top cover—An armed soldier peering out of an opening in the roof of an armoured Land Rover.
[17] VCP's—Vehicle Check Point.

[18] 'P' Checking—Personal check of identity and other documents of persons and/or motor vehicles.
[19] Big-time-players—Person(s) of Interest.
[20] R&R—Rest and Recuperation.
[21] Ulster Volunteer Force (UVF), Ulster Defence Association (UDA), Provisional Irish Republican Army (P/IRA), Irish National Liberation Army (INLA).
[22] Taig's—Term for a Catholic or Irish nationalist.
[23] Prods—Short (slang) for Protestants.
[24] Alpha-Whiskey (AW)—British army helicopter providing top cover.

Neal on AW (Alpha-Whiskey). Helicopter Patrol. Top Cover. Belfast. NI. 1987.

Neal on camp guard duty. Belfast. NI. 1987.

Neal on foot patrol. Belfast. NI. 1987.

Neal on foot patrol 2. Belfast. NI. 1987.

Neal on mobile patrol. Belfast. NI. 1987.

Y24C. Dougie, me (Neal) (rear), Rabes and Steve (front) Belfast. NI. 1987.

9. Hochzeit
(German, Wedding in English)

We had a VIP guest at our wedding and the best wedding present of all time was going to be hand-delivered 37 days later. Please read on:

Hochzeit is German for Wedding as I married a German girl and in Germany,
After 36 years together and 35 of them married, we have complete harmony.
But where and when did it all begin? Now this is a story that must be shared,
Paderborn, Germany late summer 1987, out on the town and probably impaired.
A soldier fresh from the Belfast barricades and seeing Marion in a nightclub,
For me it was love at first sight but for Marion, probably a punter in her pub?

Interim comment; Why did Frau Sauer not insist that I must learn German at school? I fobbed her off, big mistake!

It took Marion a while before she surrendered to my charm and walking her home,
Only a few weeks later when I realised, I just couldn't voluntarily leave her alone.
I am infatuated by her and the ironic thing is, is that she is ordinary, I love that,
I find that attractive, and she is tough and can hold her own and that's a fact.
Who would have thought about the future back then; a first-class Mother,
Often doing everything on her own while I was regularly away and I love her.

After only a few short but intense months, *holding hands* and completely in love,
Window-shopping at a jewellers and spotting a ring so I gave the door a shove.
Outside the shop, placing on her ring and announcing we are now engaged,
Off to McDonald's for a Big Mac as something splendid had to be celebrated.
Our family planning began in earnest and before you knew it, we were pregnant,
I asked her to marry me and she clearly accepted so I spoke with my lieutenant.

But unfortunately, attributable to England, Germany and military bureaucracy,
Our wedding day had to be delayed to just one day before Christmas (in Germany).
Christmas is a wonderful time to marry and we can't wait for our special day,
This magnificent double-bill will have a very special guest, who? I hear you say.

First and foremost, on our wedding day, we were now 8 months pregnant,
In approximately 5 weeks' time, our first baby will enter this world expectant.
Best man Keith and we couldn't do this without Anka (with little David) and Anita,
A telegram from Mum with a special message and in attendance was Oma Frieda.
Furthermore, a turnout including friends and family and receiving many presents,
The greatest gift ever will be delivered in a few short weeks, a baby presence.
But first we celebrate this union of Marion and I as we will be best friends forever,
Through good, bad, strongest and weakest times, we will be in this together.

A proud day for me, donning my army dress uniform and proud to be a soldier,
Marion will indisputably follow and support me and stand shoulder to shoulder.
You can't forget that things don't always go without some sort of caper crime,
Nipping to collect our friend Pete on our bikes rather than walk to save time.
We had had a few to drink, in half of uniform and having to give Pete a backie,
The German police stopped us but let us off under the circumstance, very lucky.

So, the special day came to an end, and now the final preparations for the baby,
And, on that day, Marion got the bus from home to barracks to meet up with me.
Perhaps we shouldn't have walked to the hospital but who was to know that,
Marion got VIP service, getting ready for the birth and even giving her a hot bath.
Saturday 28th January 1989, 37 days after our wedding day and she has arrived,
Vanessa Louise is born into this world; I was ecstatic as she moved and cried.

A long walk home with Zeppel, a rest, change of clothes and wet the baby's head,
And, finally able to bring them both home and taking Vanessa with me to bed.
Our little princess was not even one yet when we leave Germany for pastures new,
Moving to near Blackpool and managing to visit the Pleasure Beach and Beach too.
Waltzing around the house in her walker and Germany wins the World Cup in Italy,
Moving to York, Grandad moving in and her little brother Matthew is born finally.

Whilst Mum was busy with Matthew upstairs, she takes her dolly out for a walk,
After nearly calling for a helicopter to find her, she turns up and will need a talk.
The quick moves took us to Berlin for the first time and off to Spandau Kindergarten,
Sun and paddling in the pool with Matthew on the balcony and wished we had a garden.
Vanessa was very good at translating, at least in understanding what Matthew wanted,
Matthew shouting for something which translated to a biscuit, Vanessa responded.

As the British military in Berlin came to an end, we had a massive celebration,
My regiment offered subsidised flights to fly family in from the UK; our relations.
(Dean's) Linda accompanied by Russell took advantage of the offer and joined us,
All the relations were collected job lot and transported to the barracks on a bus.
Vanessa and Matthew were quite young but having family there is nice however,
We partied in the barracks and then went sightseeing in the wonderful weather.

Nearly 5, another move for a short stay in the UK and her first time on an aeroplane,
Bes goes into quarantine and Dad in his car on the ferry from Hamburg again.
Unpacked in Tidworth, Dean visiting, Vanessa off to school and time for a decision,
I was only at work for a few weeks when I was offered an overseas position.
Marion had hung the last picture when I said to her, "I have a question to ask honey,"
Do you want to stay here? Or, if you want, we can move back to Germany.

The boxes packed yet again and poor Vanessa and her little brother have no idea,
A quick stay in the UK and Vanessa is probably wondering why we can't stay here.
Arriving in Münster and attached to the REME[1], Coldstream Guards sounds posh,
Bes arrives from quarantine and LOA[2] Germany means re-earning the extra dosh.
It was great in Münster, we had a great garden and neighbours Gary and Wendy,
Vanessa was allowed outside the back gate to ride her bike which was handy.

Simba the cat here, lots of family visited from the UK and grandparents, sweet,
Vanessa's baby sister Hannah was born and with Matthew, now we are **complete**.
Technology and affordability prevailed and the Camcorder Classics began,
Dad, Gary and Steve went off to Canada and the wives partied and sang.
Vanessa nearly 8 now and we packed again and this time not far to Hohne,
Her first new friends next door especially Sebastian and his sister Francesca.

Another new school for her and Matt but they were always quick at settling in,
The school in camp had its own swimming pool and it was fun to go and swim.
Family visited in Hohne, we went to Heide Park with Linda, Carl and Sara,
We regularly visited our German family, especially Chocolate Oma and Opa.
Grandma and Bill visited often and we stayed at Winterberg and Lübbecke,
They also came with us to the Möhnesee Dam and lakes near Hannover.

The next move took us to live in Schloβ Neuhaus which was near to family,
Dad went to the Balkans again and Vanessa now 10 helping her Mum readily.
A grown-up big sister and taking part in many things at her new school,

Seeing the kids at school Christmas concerts and cam-recording was cool.
Millennium and fireworks, Grandma and Bill here to celebrate Sylvester[3],
Dad's new job a year later and a move to Köln for almost 12-year-old Vanessa.

Attending St. George's, British International School with Matt and little Hannah too,
A family affair as Mum got a job in the Reception Class so this was all new.
Only 15 months later Vanessa now 13 and we moved to Berlin for a second bout,
Being a part of the British Embassy family and we will have lots of fun no doubt.
The most stability for the kids and especially Vanessa with her important learning,
All the kids went to the Cambridge International School and they were yearning.

Times away from embassy events and school saw her mixing with her dear friends,
Understandably, as friendships blossom time without them is like your life depends.
Many of Vanessa's friends were African-American and she picked up their accent,
Unrealising, we had a Yankee in the house which was quite funny and without intent.
Holidaying in Italy a couple of times and also meeting the Duke and the Queen,
Highlights of an exemplary teenager who has worked very hard and is now sweet 16.

Grandma came over for a visit and we enjoyed sightseeing time in Berlin Mitte[4],
We mistakenly got on the train without punching our tickets and the man was bitter.
It was great when Nadina visited us and we took her visiting the local attractions,
Obviously, Dad got the grill out and it was great seeing everybody interaction.
Dad's 40th birthday bash was the final highlight of our wonderful time in Berlin,
Friends and colleagues from the embassy joining in with the festivities within.

Off to JHQ[5] for Dad's last job in the army and Vanessa's final year of high school,
JHQ had plenty to offer, a military town with schools, shops, a cinema and a pool.
Extending our time there so Vanessa could go into sixth form which she relished,
Time overall, with all the learning and leaving school with high grades she cherished.
Vanessa's first job at 18 saw her at retail at the NAAFI[6], earning her own cash,
At weekends, she would venture into Mönchengladbach with her friends on the lash.

Leaving home and off to the UK with her boyfriend and Matt went to Army College,
They know best when they leave home for adventures with their new knowledge.
Never stepping in her way and after a few years, she came back to the mothership,
Back in Germany and back to school learning German and then an apprenticeship.
Life goes fast when you are having fun, qualified, working hard and getting hitched,
Vanessa has 2 beautiful children and she is everything we could have wished.

[1] REME—Royal Electrical and Mechanical Engineers.
[2] LOA—Living Overseas Allowance.
[3] Sylvester—Is the German name for New Year's Eve.
[4] Berlin Mitte—The centre of Berlin.
[5] JHQ—Joint Headquarters, Mönchengladbach.
[6] NAAFI—Navy, Army and Air Force Institutes.

Anka (David), Neal, Marion, Keith at our wedding 23.12.1988.

Neal and Marion at our wedding 23.12.1988.

Marion (Mum) with Vanessa.

Neal (Dad) with Vanessa.

Marion (Mum) with Vanessa.

Vanessa with her grandma.

Vanessa with her baby sister Hannah.

Vanessa age 9.

Vanessa and Matt.

Vanessa age 12.

10. Straight Shooter

I did not volunteer to be a sniper but I was a good shot,
A late German autumn crack of dawn summoned us weary lot.
Donning our ghillie suits; embroidered camouflage clothing,
You couldn't see out properly and we were already loathing.

Our first training mission was to crawl literary on our fronts,
For what seemed hours, we quietly grunt and silently shunt.
After a couple of a hundred metres, with space in-between,
One by one, we were picked off by an observer unseen.

I was still hidden, crawling through brooks, cold and wet,
Moving slowly and stealthily, avoiding detection and the threat.
Unknowingly all alone, I ponder that the rest were caught,
I continued patiently, using the banks as cover, as I was taught.

After an eternity, the observer shouted out, "Neal, show your face,"
I proudly stood up to be seen and realised I had won this tortoise race.
The next mission was the shooting ranges and take out the targets,
In prone position with rifle and encircled by the spotter Instructors.

Looking through the telescopic sight and controlling my breathing,
Taking a mental note of the wind speed and direction and adjusting.
A few hundred metres away it is hard to make out the form and shape,
This wooden target had nowhere to run and there was no escape.

The target might only sit there and stare or move left and right,
The idea of the sniper is to avoid the physical battle, the fight.
In real life, the target is the enemy and you should never be spotted,
Or else you will not be there for the next shot as you could be slotted.

Being one of the best shots and not being seen on the stalk,
I thought I passed this gruelling cadre, until I had the talk.
"My attitude spoiled my chance," said Lead Instructor Jack[1],
"I know I am a straight shooter, Sir, and would have had your back."

Sniper Cadre autumn, Paderborn, Germany.

---

[1] Unfortunately, Jack died sometime later. RIP.

11. It's a Boy

Married with a lovely little girl Vanessa, and too, every man wants his little boy,
I suppose, in a way, we can do man-things, something every dad can enjoy.
But you are 2 weeks late, Son, why the hell do UK hospitals leave it so late?
Waiting and waiting, back to and from the hospital in York, a date is a date.

Sunday 12th May 1991, Matthew is welcomed into the world and very overdue,
Waiting for this day was tormenting and leaving them in the hospital was too.
My dad was staying with us for a while and he was already a top grandad,
Dad was so looking forward to meeting his new grandson, he was so glad.

Visiting them and breaking down was not part of the plan and very annoyed,
Visited by his grandad and big sister Vanessa and everyone was so overjoyed.
Matthew was going through a hard time in hospital and was always crying,
Dislocating his shoulder during his birth so his pain must have been un-denying.

Healing and home, ready to start living and enjoying being part of the litter,
A welcoming full house of love, with all of us and not forgetting our babysitter.
Grandad moving out into his static mobile home gave us the space we need,
He missed taking Bes for walks but he was happy, something we all agreed.

Grandad moving back to Burnley and we are off to Germany's capital city,
Back to the Lancashire lads in Berlin and aren't those Buddy Bears[1] pretty?
Little ones; Vanessa and toddler Matthew in the paddling pool on the balcony,
Summer is hot and paddling pools are the obvious choice of the day, totally.

Not forgetting his German family and 'Chocolate Oma'[2] was smitten,
She couldn't pronounce his name bless her, even showing her, it written.
'Matt' interpreted, means meat, so that didn't sit well with her either,
Nevertheless, she tried and she was regarded as the best Oma ever.

After a few short weeks living in the UK, we are returning to Germany,
Münster welcomed us, a lovely garden and perfect for children, absolutely.
On the water-slide in summer was perfect and Vanessa was in the pool,
And, the dad and son things start to bond and we were acting the fool.

Little Hannah was born but her and Vanessa have separate pages,
Big sister and brother playing out with their friends and not seen for ages.
Budding into a top boy and a very proud big brother to his new little sister,
He loved his big brother duties with Hannah and he always protected her.

Grandad came over to visit us so we are off to the airport to collect him,
When he saw his grandson again, he was ecstatic, it's a man-thing.
The men spent so much time together, taking Bes out for long walks,
Bes swimming in the lake, Matthew on the death-slide and many talks.
Grandad used to call him "Matt the bat, with a hat, I'm not."—It stuck!

Next stop Hohne and then to Schloß Neuhaus near to our German family,
His Onkel, Frank loves Matthew and when he was a young boy especially.
Matthew saved his cousin Frauke from getting seriously hurt one day,
So injured Matthew will always be a hero for that day, Frank would say.

I was away a lot when Matthew was growing up so he was promoted,
Matt was the man of the house now in place of his dad, who duly noted.
Looking after his mum and sisters with ease and being so proud of himself,
I would tell him thank you on the phone or in a note of sorts and also proud myself.

Our next move detached from BFG[3] (sort of) and off to exclusive Köln,
He loved his year at St. George's—The British International School Köln.
Inline skating in front of the Dom was a highlight he will never forget,
His knack and new-found balance rollerblading mustered up a sweat.

Berlin again and he loved his Eminem and his gangster friends,
Holidaying in Italy[4] and playing frisbee and basketball with no end.
A teenager and doing very well in school and we were so proud,
Even singing at the school play was memorable and he was so loud.

He enjoyed being part of the embassy family and including other nations,
A pupil at the Cambridge International School gave him a good foundation.
Invited to a friend's birthday party, and something we have never seen,
Negotiating the turns, his friends for the party picked him up in a limousine.

His last two years school was Windsor School in Joint Headquarters,
Living near to Mönchengladbach, but not really Borussia supporters.
His 16th birthday on the ranges shooting handguns and nearly falling back,
I beat him on a street race and he beat me on a 10-mile marathon track.

In his time at Windsor School, he sampled rugby with the Rhinos,
The Joint Headquarters Mini Rhinos match was won by who knows.
It was taking part that counts, just like his days playing football,
Man of the match with Paderborn United made him rightly stand tall.

Before Matt left us for the Army Apprentices College Harrogate,
He asked me, "can we do something, Dad, something big, mate?"
Mosel River Expedition, the boys cycling 200 km from Trier to Koblenz,
Over 3 days and 2 nights camping and a newspaper article made sense.

"Time for the off, Son," to go to the college in Harrogate, road-trip day,
Dad and Son driving alone to the UK and visiting family on the way.
Leaving him there alone was hard but I knew he would be looked after,
I will see him in a few weeks and will take him back home to laughter.

Matt graduated from the college and it was a very honoured day for us all,
We all drove over from Germany for this very proud day and we had a ball.
After the year at Harrogate and leave in Germany, off for Royal Engineer training,
He will be a military engineer and as a design draughtsman, finally attaining.

Matt endured 2 tours of Afghanistan and in-between exercising in Kenya too,
The time he spent in Afghanistan was very hard and the bravest thing to do.
Not one member in the whole family has ever done anything like that,
We were very scared for him and he came home safe and I take off my hat.

Having left the army after his time on tour, he had had enough,
The army wasn't for him in the end, but he had it really rough.
Making it on civvy street[5] is something else he should boast about,
Living with Emma in the UK and he will do very well, I have no doubt.

---

[1] Buddy Bears—Since their inception, the Berlin Buddy Bears have been committed to peaceful coexistence between people of different origins, cultures and religions. The likeable ambassadors of a cosmopolitan Berlin have become a symbol of tolerance and

international understanding through a variety of different projects. But their mission goes beyond promoting global dialogue: they stand up for sustainable approach that has the future of our world in mind. Through initiatives, the Buddy Bears contribute to creating awareness for sustainable action while supporting children in need. Because peace, respect and tolerance start with a sustainable concern for our planet and all its inhabitants.

[2] 'Chocolate Oma' was his German great-grandmother, they called her this name as she always had chocolate and sweets for the kids.

[3] BFG—British Forces Germany.

[4] Lake Garda, Italy (thrice).

[5] People in the armed forces use civvy street to refer to life and work which is not connected with armed forces.

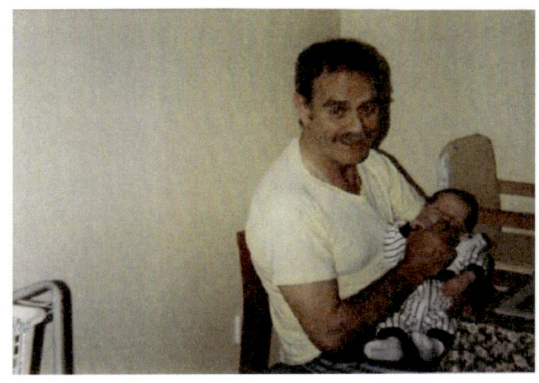

Matthew and his grandad May 1991.

Oma (great-grandmother), Vanessa and Matthew 1992.

Matthew posing on a wooden plane 1992/93?

Matthew and his mum, Marion.

Matthew and his sister Hannah.

Matthew: Man of the Match.

Matthew and family, British Embassy Berlin state visit, November 2004.

Neal (Dad) front, Matthew took the photograph Mosel, Germany 2007.

Matthew in Afghanistan 2011.

To mark his son embarking upon a career in the army, SSgt Neal ▇▇▇▇ planned a challenging bike ride along the Mosel river cycle route. In this article he reflects on the trip and his feelings as he watches Matthew follow in his footsteps.

by SSgt ▇▇▇▇▇▇
Media & Comms BFG

AFTER serving for almost 23 years in the Army, I am delighted that my son Matthew (16) is following my footsteps into a most rewarding career. I am extra proud of the fact that he leaves school with many more qualifications than I achieved when I left school and that he is joining the Royal Engineers, whereas before I transferred to the Adjutant Generals Corps I enlisted into the infantry.

Matthew left Windsor School in Rheindahlen having gained high GCSE results in nine subjects including an A grade in German, four grade Bs in other subjects and a Double B Award for Science. Attributable to his high grades, Matthew has been accepted into the army as an apprentice and commenced training at the Army Foundation College, Harrogate, as a Royal Engineer (Design Draftsman) on September 9.

Matthew is a keen sportsman. He played for the Under 17s Rhino's Rugby Team until he left school and, having participated in the Brüggen 10 Road Race with me last year, asked me if we could do something of this magnitude before he departed for the UK as a "build-up for his fitness". I participated in Exercise Mosel Marathon last year, UKSC(G)'s team development event, a cycling event from Koblenz to Schweich along the Mosel River cycle route and decided to utilise that trip as the recce for cycling it again this year. On this occasion, however, we would cycle almost 200km in the opposite direction.

EXPEDITION

After studying the maps together, he was not deterred and, to make it more like an expedition, we would do the trip without the usual drop-off transport and comfy hotels instead taking the train to the start point and overnight in a tent.

We left home in Erkelenz at 4.30am on the packed bikes and cycled to the train station to board our train to Trier. Once in Trier we set off on the gruelling trip at 10am following the green arrows (cycle route markers), aiming to cover the journey in three days.

We lunched at Detzem (30km) and stopped for the night at a campsite at Lieser near Bernkastel-Kues (34km). That evening we joined in the local wine festival still managing to get an early night.

On day two we set off at 10am for our second (and hardest) day in the saddle. The warm temperatures helped our strength and the pleasantness of passing other cyclists and swapping hellos was rewarding. We enjoyed our lunch in Zell (44km) and finally stopped for the night in Fankel, just south of Cochem (30km). And, what do you know, the town was enjoying their annual Weinfest. Naturally we joined in with the festivities but again crawled to bed before midnight.

Day three felt easier and was good for morale thinking that we could go home for a proper shower and sleep in a comfy bed on the completion of the day. After lunch in Kobern-Gondorf (32km) we cycled on to Koblenz and the end of the journey, or so we thought. A Sunday market blocked our route and we were forced to detour through the city centre to the Deutsches Eck which was exhausting. After a break and taking some photographs we caught the train home. In Erkelenz we were tired but still managed to cycle the final 6km home.

Matt often remarked on the fantastic views of the vast vineyards and many castles and kept a smile on his face throughout the trip. Both of us would recommend a visit to the Mosel to anyone. What an achievement. Well done Matt!

● A brief pause to admire the sights before moving on to complete the long ride

12. Cold War

Roosevelt and Stalin agreed that a defeated Germany should be split into two,
The German Democratic Republic and The German Federal Republic debut.
The Berlin Blockade and Airlift in 1948–49 and NATO[1] formed in 1949,
NATO's founding members in Europe, Canada and the United States combine.
Obviously, Berlin was at the forefront of the Cold War when it was sadly divided,
East Berlin the Soviet Sector, West Berlin the French, British and American united.
The Wall was erected on 13th August 1961 and the first of its kind to divide a nation,
It was a 155 km barrier enclosing West Berlin which separated a population.

The Cold War was from 12th March 1947 until Christmas Day 1991,
The Soviet Union collapsed and 15 newly independent nations were born.
In all honesty, I have little to nothing to do with the Cold War as such,
Joining my regiment spring 1985 and in Germany but that is not much.
Officially, the time period of around 1985–1991* marked the final period and,
The Cold War was coming to a natural end as peace was very much in hand.
Geopolitical tensions between the Soviet and US-led blocs were easing,
The collapse of the Soviet Union's influence in Eastern Europe was pleasing.

So, for the 6 years mentioned (above)*, my time saw me training as a soldier,
Training was geared around the possibility of the war becoming colder.
A different context to begin with, winter 1984 in Germany was severe,
My regiment were on manoeuvres in Soltau[2], North Germany that year.
It was talked about for many years as the coldest exercise ever,
I joined the following year and winter 1985 was also bitterly cold however.
We seemed to be on manoeuvres constantly, readying for a battle,
Travelling on the overnight train to Soltau as though we were cattle.

Mock battles in the thick woods, trench warfare and firing blanks,
And, on occasion, perhaps the final annual exercise, training with tanks.
Up all night in sometimes extremely cold temperatures on sentry,
Watching forward and left and right of arc and password for entry.
Squads of soldiers, full kit and weapons marching[3] to the ranges,

Shooting[4] the pop-up targets down range when it changes.
I trained in many weapons including the L16 81mm mortar,
BRIXMIS[5] versus SOXMIS[6] was primarily what it was all for.

Even in the warmth of barracks, we were always training for the possibility,
Learning Soviet armoured fighting vehicles and aircraft recognition in case of hostility.
Always ensuring our soldiers and our armoured fighting vehicles were warring fit,
On the off-chance things did not go down well and we would have to do our bit.
Even deploying to Canada so that we could carry out more live-firing training,
Joining up with armoured tank regiments so that the battlegroup is sustaining.
Some of us guarding a section of the vast 1,381 km inner German borders,
Patrolling the Hertz mountains and protecting the 'Berliner' military train were orders.

Sadly, my regiment left Germany just before the immense celebrations,
9th November 1989 falling of the Berlin Wall during a Peaceful Revolution.
It did not end there though for the regiment's involvement in the transition,
Berlin was still drawing down and our task was the draw down mission.
My regiment returned to Germany's capital, Berlin in 1992, to Spandau,
Interesting times ahead and the nearby Soviet barracks is empty now.
It seemed only Allied troops were here now and it was all coming to an end,
There were retired Soviet soldiers potted about and I even made a new friend.

In commemoration, this short story was purposely initiated on 9th November 2023.

Touring the centre and parts of the Wall and the memorials of the suffering,
Berlin was lively, celebrations and remembrance seemed to still be in full swing.
Parts of the famous Spandau Prison were now a NAAFI[7] shopping centre,
It's last prisoner, Rudolf Hess died on 17th August 1987 in the prison there.
Brandenburg Gate was the obvious centre of attraction for tourism,
Although this prestige place was transforming away from communism.
Not far from the Checkpoint Charlie[8] American guard house that is still there,
American soldiers (but probably veterans or civilians) enthusiastically stare.

In my first time in Berlin in 1992, was such an experience, Berlin Mitte,
Pariser Platz was transforming from nothing to something and there is no litter.
Embassies were slowly erecting as Berlin has been the new capital since 1990,
Passing the existing Russian Embassy west and the Brandenburg Gate was mighty.
On the other side of the Gate, the Quadriga[9] symbolising peace entering the city,

The many trees with flowers along the Straβe des 17. Juni looks very pretty.
There are remains of the Wall throughout the city, largely along the Spree[10],
A modern square in no man's land at Potsdamer Platz is a future to see.

1992–94 and times were good for the brits in their (now fully open) sector of Berlin,
We had the boroughs of, Charlottenburg, Spandau, Wilmersdorf and Tiergarten.
The Olympic Stadium was on our patch and I stood on the steps where **he** stood,
'Stood on the steps opening the 1936 Olympic Games before **he** spilled that blood.'
I actually ran into the crowded stadium on completion of the 25km Berlin marathon,
We swam our military swim test there in the adjacent Olympic pools in the sun.
Prince Charles visited and we gave him a parade which was followed by a party,
Many pop stars gave us a concert and we opened the place for the public to see.

18th June[11] 1994 was the beginning of the end as we formed for the Allied Parade,
This extraordinary drill spectacle was the hardest parade I have ever made.
The French, British and American contingents and my regiment led the British,
Marching the Straβe des 17. Juni, and around the Victory Column[12] to the finish[13].
The programme was full of much to see, including parachutists and the flypasts,
Helicopters, Berlin's motorcycle police, a Dakota aircraft and many military bands.
Ceremony of honour, gun salutes and the inspection of thousands of personnel,
The formations had done their nations proud and gave Berlin a good farewell.

Closing note from the poet: I returned to Berlin in 2002 (-2005), as a soldier and part of the British embassy staff. The embassy (adjoining the Adlon Hotel) on Wilhelmstraβe was opened by HM Queen Elizabeth II on 18th July 2000. Just around the corner from Wilhelmstraβe, Parizer Platz is now complete with embassies and other famous prominent buildings and the Adlon Hotel. The new United States Embassy[14] is being built on Parizer Platz practically adjoining the Brandenburg Gate. No man's land at Potsdamer Platz is now full of prestige buildings, shopping precincts, cinemas and much more to see.

---

[1] NATO—The North Atlantic Treaty Organisation.
[2] Soltau is a mid-sized town in the Lüneburg Heath in the district of Heidekreis, in Lower Saxony. Military training areas.
[3] Marching—in this case, marching but mostly jogging as it was primarily a proper competition (March and Shoot Competition).
[4] Live-firing.
[5] BRIXMIS—British Commanders'-in-Chief Mission to the Soviet Forces in Germany.

[6] SOXMIS—Soviet Exercise Mission (Soviet Military observers in West Germany during cold war era).

[7] NAAFI—Navy, Army, and Air Force Institutes.

[8] Checkpoint Charlie—Was the best-known Berlin Wall crossing point between East Berlin and West Berlin during the Cold War, as named by the Western Allies.

[9] Quadriga—The Quadriga was placed on top of the Brandenburg Gate by Johann Gottfried Schadow in 1793. The sculpture, depicting a two-wheeled chariot pulled by four horses running side by side, was meant to symbolise peace entering the city.

[10] Spree—The Spree (river) with a length of approximately 400 kilometres (250 miles) flows through Berlin's city centre.

[11] 18th June—This is very fitting to celebrate this day with this substantial parade. I have a feeling that the date was chosen by my Regiment on purpose. 18th June 1815, The Battle of Waterloo is the most significant Battle Honour for my Regiment, The Queen's Lancashire Regiment.

[12] The Victory Column (Siegessäule) is a monument designed by Heinrich Strack after 1864 to commemorate the Prussian victory in the Second Schleswig War.

[13] Approximately 4km march.

[14] The Embassy of the United States of America (Former U.S. Chancery was relocated from Neustädtische Kirchstrasse to Pariser Platz) was opened in 2008.

On Cold War Military Training 1/3.

On Cold War Military Training 2/3.

On Cold War Military Training 3/3.

Allied Parade 1/2—18 Jun 94.

Allied Parade 2/2—18 Jun 94.

PARADE
der Alliierten Streitkräfte in Berlin
18. Juni 1994 10.00 –12.00 Uhr · Straße des 17. Juni
Zwischen Charlottenburger Tor und Kleinem Stern

Presse- und
Informationsamt
des
Landes Berlin

THANK YOU MERCI DANKESCHÖN

PARADE DER ALLIIERTEN STREITKRÄFTE IN BERLIN

18. Juni 1994 · 10.00 - 12.00 · Straße des 17. Juni
Zwischen Charlottenburger Tor und Kleinem Stern

Général Brullard · Major General Yates · Brigadier Bromhead

Eberhard DIEPGEN
Regierender Bürgermeister von Berlin
Governing Mayor of Berlin
Bourgmestre régnant de Berlin

Fast 50 Jahre lang gehörten die Soldaten der alliierten Schutzmächte zum Berliner Leben. Zunächst als Besatzungsmacht, seit der Blockade unserer Stadt und der Luftbrücke als Verbündete und Freunde. Viele Freundschaften zwischen Amerikanern, Briten, Franzosen und Berlinern sind in den vergangenen Jahrzehnten gewachsen. Sie sind ein gutes Fundament für unsere weiteren Beziehungen und die Westbindung Deutschlands.
Bei dieser letzten militärischen Zeremonie, der Abschiedsparade, ist ein bißchen Wehmut mit dabei. Eine Epoche geht unwiederbringlich zu Ende. Freunde verlassen unsere Stadt.
Wir Berliner sagen von Herzen: Lebewohl! Danke! Aber vor allem: Auf Wiedersehen!

For almost fifty years the forces of the Allied Protecting Powers have been part of the life of Berlin. First as occupation powers, since the Blockade of our city and the Air Lift as allies and friends. Many friendships between Americans, Britons, French and Berliners have grown up during the past decades. They are a good basis for our future relations and Germany's ties to the west.
There is a certain sadness associated with this last military ceremony, the Farewell Parade. An era is coming to its irrevocable end. Friends are leaving our city.
We Berliners say from our hearts: Farewell! Thank you! But above all: Auf Wiedersehen!

Pendant près de cinquante ans, les soldats des Forces de protection Alliées ont fait partie de la vie de Berlin. Tout d'abord en tant que puissances occupantes, puis en alliés et amis depuis le Blocus de notre ville et le Pont aérien.
De nombreuses amitiés se sont développées au cours des décennies passées entre les Américains, les Britanniques, les Français et les Allemands. Elles sont un bon fondement pour la poursuite de nos relations et l'ancrage de l'Allemagne à l'Ouest.
Cette dernière cérémonie militaire, la revue d'adieu, s'accompagne d'une certaine mélancolie. Un époque s'achève irrémédiablement. Ce sont des amis qui quittent notre ville.
Nous autres Berlinois vous disons de tout coeur: adieu! Merci! Mais surtout: Auf Wiedersehen!

Général Jean BRULLARD
C.F.F.S.B.
Kommandant der in Berlin stationierten Französischen Streitkräfte
Commandant of the French Forces Stationed in Berlin

Chers amis et amies de Berlin,
c'est aujourd'hui un immense honneur et un réel plaisir pour les hommes et les femmes des Forces Françaises stationnées à Berlin d'avoir la chance de défiler une dernière fois au cœur de Berlin, entourés par une population qui leur est chère.
Que soient remerciés ici tous ceux qui, par leur volonté et leurs efforts, ont permis qu'un tel événement ait lieu.
Je salue à cette occasion les autorités de la ville. Je salue également nos frères d'armes des Etats-Unis et de Grande Bretagne. Je salue enfin et surtout l'ensemble des Berlinois qui, pendant quarante neuf ans, nous a soutenu dans cette mission de défense de la Liberté.
Bonne chance à tous les Berlinois et AU REVOIR.

Liebe Freunde und Freundinnen in Berlin,
für die Männer und Frauen der in Berlin stationierten Französischen Streitkräfte ist es heute eine außerordentliche Ehre und eine echte Freude, die Gelegenheit zu haben, zum letzten Mal durch das Herz von Berlin zu marschieren, inmitten einer Bevölkerung, die sie liebgewonnen haben.
Herzlichen Dank an alle, die mit viel Willenskraft und Mühe ein derartiges Ereignis ermöglicht haben.
Ich grüße bei dieser Gelegenheit die Behörden der Stadt Berlin. Ich grüße auch unsere Waffenbrüder aus den Vereinigten Staaten und Großbritannien. Ich grüße schließlich und ganz besonders alle Berliner, die uns neunundvierzig Jahre lang bei der Aufgabe, die Freiheit zu schützen, unterstützt haben.
Allen Berlinern viel Glück und AU REVOIR.

Dear friends of Berlin,
It is a great honour and a real pleasure for the men and women of the French Forces stationed in Berlin to have the opportunity today to march for one last time in the heart of Berlin, surrounded by a population they hold dear.
I should like to thank all those who, through their goodwill and efforts, have made such an event possible.
I take this opportunity to salute the city authorities. I also salute our brothers in arms from the USA and Great Britain who, over forty-nine years, have supported us in our mission of the defence of liberty.
I wish all the Berliners the best of luck and AU REVOIR.

Brigadier David BROMHEAD
Commander Berlin Infantry Brigade
Kommandeur der Britischen Infantriebrigade in Berlin
Général Commandant la Berlin Infantry Brigade

Major General Walter H. YATES
Commander, United States Army Berlin
Kommandant United States Army Berlin
Commandant, United States Army Berlin

The Berlin Infantry Brigade and Royal Air Force Gatow are delighted to be able to participate in the Allied Farewell Parade today. Before we leave your city later this year after 49 years, this Parade gives us the opportunity, together with our Allies, to say goodbye to the people of Berlin and to thank you for the way in which you have made us so welcome.
The culmination of our presence here has only been achieved by a joint effort between the Allies, the city authorities and the people of Berlin. It is my sincere hope that the strong friendships that have built up over the years will continue into the future, but in the meantime we are all indebted to you for your kindness and wonderful support; thank you and goodbye.

Die Berlin Infantry Brigade und die Royal Air Force Gatow freuen sich, heute an der Alliierten Abschiedsparade teilnehmen zu können. Bevor wir nach 49 Jahren noch in diesem Jahr Ihre Stadt verlassen, bietet uns diese Parade Gelegenheit, uns gemeinsam mit unseren Verbündeten von den Berlinern zu verabschieden und uns bei Ihnen dafür zu bedanken, daß Sie uns das Gefühl gaben, willkommen zu sein.
Der Höhepunkt unserer Anwesenheit hier wurde nur durch gemeinsames Vorgehen der Alliierten, der Berliner Behörden und der Berliner Bevölkerung möglich. Ich hoffe sehr, daß die starken freundschaftlichen Bande, die sich im Laufe der Jahre herausgebildet haben, auch künftig weiterbestehen. Vorerst stehen wir aber in Ihrer Schuld für Ihre Freundlichkeit und großartige Unterstützung. Vielen Dank und Auf Wiedersehen.

La Brigade d'Infanterie de Berlin et la Royal Air Force Gatow sont heureux de participer aujourd'hui à la revue d'adieu des Alliés. Avant de quitter votre ville dans quelques mois, après 49 années, cette revue nous donne l'occasion de dire, avec nos alliés, au-revoir au peuple de Berlin et de vous remercier pour la façon dont vous nous avez accueillis.
L'apogée de notre présence ici n'a pu s'accomplir que grâce à un effort conjoint entre les Alliés, les autorités de la ville et les Berlinois. J'espère sincèrement que l'étroite amitié qui s'est construite pendant toutes ces années se poursuivra à l'avenir, mais d'ici là nous vous exprimons notre reconnaissance pour votre gentillesse et votre magnifique soutien. Merci, et au revoir.

Through the years a special bond has developed between Americans and the people of Berlin. Together we have faced dark, perilous days, and we have shared the joy of reuniting families, cities and a nation.
It has been an honor to serve in Berlin. Nowhere else has the West more clearly demonstrated its resolve to deter aggression, promote democracy and protect freedom.
Our mission is complete; it is time to leave. Yet, Berlin has been a home away from home for thousands of Americans. Leaving is not easy, but we hope to leave a legacy of freedom, hope, goodwill and tolerance.
Our best wishes to you all. Auf Wiedersehen!

Im Laufe der Jahre hat sich zwischen den Amerikanern und den Berlinern eine besondere Verbundenheit entwickelt. Gemeinsam haben wir dunkle Tage der Gefahr durchlitten, und gemeinsam haben wir die Freude der Wiedervereinigung von Familien, Städten und einer Nation erlebt.
Es war eine Ehre, in Berlin zu dienen. Nirgendwo sonst hat der Westen deutlicher seine Entschlossenheit bekundet, die Aggression abzuwehren, die Demokratie zu stärken und die Freiheit zu schützen.
Unsere Mission ist beendet; es ist Zeit zu gehen. Doch für Tausende von Amerikanern ist Berlin zur zweiten Heimat geworden. Der Abschied fällt nicht leicht, aber wir haben die Hoffnung, daß wir als unser Erbe Freiheit, Hoffnung, Wohlwollen und Toleranz zurücklassen.
Alles Gute für Sie alle. Auf Wiedersehen!

Pendant des années, un lien spécial s'est développé entre les Américains et les gens de Berlin. Ensemble, nous avons fait face à des jours sombres, dangereux, et nous avons partagé la joie des familles, des villes et d'une nation réunifiées.
Servir à Berlin a été un honneur. Nulle part ailleurs l'Ouest n'a démontré avec autant de clarté sa détermination à résister à l'agression, à promouvoir la démocratie et à protéger la liberté.
Notre mission est accomplie; le temps de partir est venu. Berlin a été, loin de chez eux, un foyer pour des milliers d'Américains. Partir n'est pas facile mais nous espérons laisser un héritage de paix, d'espoir, de bonne volonté et de tolérance.
Nos meilleurs vœux à vous tous. Auf Wiedersehen!

PARADE INTERALLIEE

Forces Françaises défilant
Französische Teilnehmer der Parade
French Forces Marching

ALLIED PARADE

British Parade Personnel
Britische Teilnehmer der Parade
Troupes Britannique

- Musique des Forces Françaises stationnées en Allemagne, Chef de Musique: Capitaine Mouginot
- Musique du 46e Régiment d'Infanterie, Chef de Musique: Adjudant Fleck
- Colonel Commandant les Troupes Françaises: Colonel Rousselet
- Officier Français Commandant la Garde aux Couleurs Tripartite Chef de Bataillon Hahn
- Gendarmerie
- Base Aérienne 165 (Air Force), Chef de Corps: Colonel Pepin
- 46e Régiment d'Infanterie, Chef de Corps: Colonel Buttay
- 11e Régiment de Chasseurs, Chef de Corps: Lt-Colonel Chanoine
- Groupement de soutien, Chef de Corps: Lt-Colonel Fromager
- Détachement de Quartier Général, Chef de Détachement: Chef d'Escadron Mourot

Commanding Officer First Battalion The Queen's Own Lancashire Regiment: Lieutenant Colonel G H P Flood MBE QLR

- No 1 Guard Commander, The Queen's Lancashire Regiment: Major J F Lloyd QLR
- No 2 Guard Commander, The Queen's Lancashire Regiment: Major I A N Urquhart KING'S OWN BORDER
- No 3 Guard Commander, The Queen's Lancashire Regiment: Major D J Sanderson MBE QLR
- No 4 Guard Commander, Berlin Brigade Support Units: Major A R Law RLC
- No 5 Guard Commander, Berlin Brigade Support Units: Major W Powell R SIGNALS
- No 6 Guard Commander, Royal Air Force Sqn Ldr E J Adey RAF
- No 7 Guard Commander, Royal Air Force Sqn Ldr A Campbell RAF

Tripartite Colour Guard:
- Officer of the British Guard: Lieutenant D C Todd QLR
- British National Flag Carrier: Lt R Cartwright QLR
- Tripartite Colour Guard RSM: WO1 (RSM) Gresty Cheshire

Parachutists:
- Members of the PRINCESS OF WALES's ROYAL REGIMENT's freefall parachute display team "THE TIGERS" led by Lieutenant NM Reid, PWRR

Bands:
- The Regimental Band of the 2nd Royal Tank Regiment
- The Regimental Band of the Irish Guards
- The Pipes and Drums of the 1st Battalion The Royal Highland Fusiliers
- The Regimental Band and Corps of Drums 1st Battalion The Queen's Lancashire Regiment
- The Regimental Pipes and Drums of the 3rd Battalion The Royal Irish Regiment
- The Band of the Air Force Germany

ALLIED PARADE

U.S. Forces (Units in Order of Marching)
US-Streitkräfte (Einheiten in der Reihenfolge des Aufmarsches)
Forces américaines
(Unités par ordre de marche)

- Headquarters, Berlin Brigade - Colonel Jimmy C. Banks
- 298th Army Band - Chief Warrant Officer 3 Larry G. Hyatt
- 5th Battalion-502d Infantry Regiment - Lieutenant Colonel Joseph O. Rodriguez
- 6th Battalion-502d Infantry Regiment - Lieutenant Colonel Walter L. Holton
- 76th U.S. Army Band - Chief Warrant Officer 2 Kenneth D. Allen
- Combat Support Battalion - Lieutenant Colonel Gordon D. Weith
- Community Activity Battalion - Lieutenant Colonel James C. Whitmire (consisting of Army Medical Department; Headquarters, United States Military Community Activity & 287th Military Police Company)

BUNDESWEHR

- Standortkommandant Brigadegeneral Hasso Freiherr von Uslar-Gleichen
- Luftwaffenmusikkorps 4 unter der Leitung von Oberstleutnant Bernd Ziffny

PROGRAMM

Ab 10.00 Uhr werden die Zuschauer entlang der Straße des 17. Juni unterhalten durch:

- Fallschirmspringer der Alliierten
- Berlin Brigade Drill Team
- Queen's Colour Squadron Drill Team
- Luftwaffenmusikkorps 4 unter der Leitung von Oberstleutnant Bernd Ziffny
- Orchester der Berliner Polizei unter Leitung vom Ersten Polizeihauptkommissar Michael Kern
- Motorradsportgruppe der Berliner Polizei unter der Leitung von Polizeihauptkommissar Georg Franke

Sprecher: Hans-Heinrich Isenbart

Zeit	Ablauf	Hinweise für die Zuschauer
11.00	Ankunft der Kommandanten der französischen, britischen und amerikanischen Truppen und des deutschen Standortkommandanten Ankunft des Regierenden Bürgermeisters von Berlin	Erheben sich
11.03	Ehrenzeremoniell mit Salutschüssen	Stehen während der Musik
11.10	Abnahme der alliierten Formation	
11.15	Hissen der vier Nationalfahnen	Stehen während der Nationalhymnen
11.20	Rede des Regierenden Bürgermeisters	
11.35	• Helikopter-Vorbeiflug • Ehrengarde der drei Alliierten • Vorbeimarsch der Orchester und Truppenverbände • Reiter der Polizei • Vorbeiflug einer Dakota	Erheben sich beim Vorbeimarsch der National- und Regimentsfahnen
12.05	Abfahrt des Regierenden Bürgermeisters und der Kommandanten Einholen der Nationalfahnen	Erheben sich

PROGRAMME

From 10.00 a.m. onwards spectators along the Strasse des 17. Juni will be entertained by:

- Allied parachutists
- Berlin Brigade Drill Team
- Queen's Colour Squadron Drill Team
- Luftwaffenmusikkorps 4 conducted by Oberstleutnant Bernd Ziffny
- Berliner Polizei Orchestra conducted by Erster Polizeihauptkommissar Michael Kern
- Motorcycle Sport Group of the Berliner Polizei under Polizeihauptkommissar Georg Franke

Narrator: Hans-Heinrich Isenbart

Time	Events	Instructions for Spectators
11.00 a.m.	Arrival of the Commanders of the French, British and American Forces and the German Commander Arrival of the Governing Mayor of Berlin	Stand
11.03 a.m.	Ceremony of honour with gun salute	Stand during the music
11.10 a.m.	Inspection of the Allied formation	
11.15 a.m.	Hoisting of the four national flags	Stand during the national anthems
11.20 a.m.	Speech by the Governing Mayor	
11.35 a.m.	• Helicopter flypast • Guards of honour of the three Allies • March past of the bands and troops • Mounted police • Flypast of a Dakota	Stand during the march past of the national and regimental flags
12.05 p.m.	Departure of the Governing Mayor and Commanders Lowering of the national flags	Stand

PROGRAMME

A partir de 10 h, les spectateurs se tenant sur la Strasse des 17. Juni pourront assister aux prestations des groupes suivants:

- Parachutistes alliés
- Berlin Brigade Drill Team
- Queen's Colour Squadron Drill Team
- Corps de musique 4 de la Luftwaffe sous la direction du lieutenant-colonel Bernd Ziffny
- Orchestre de la police berlinoise sous la direction du Premier commissaire de police principal Michael Kern
- Groupe de sport motocycliste de la police berlinoise sous la direction du commissaire de police principal Georg Franke

Narrateur: Hans-Heinrich Isenbart

heure	déroulement	directives pour les spectateurs
11 h 00	Arrivée des commandants des troupes françaises, britanniques et américaines et du commandant allemand de la place Arrivée du Bourgmestre régnant de Berlin	se lèvent
11 h 03	Cérémonie des honneurs avec salve d'honneur	restent debout pendant la musique
11 h 10	Passage en revue de la formation alliée	
11 h 15	Lever des quatre drapeaux nationaux	restent debout pendant que sont joués les hymnes nationaux
11 h 20	Allocution du Bourgmestre régnant	
11 h 35	• Survol d'hélicoptères • Garde aux couleurs tripartites • Défilé des orchestres et des corps de troupe • Police montée • Survol d'un Dakota	se lèvent lorsque passent les couleurs nationales et les drapeaux des régiments
12 h 05	Départ du Bourgmestre régnant et des commandants Baisser des drapeaux nationaux	se lèvent

STATIONEN EINER FREUNDSCHAFT
MILESTONES OF A FRIENDSHIP
STATIONS D'UNE AMITIÉ

1961

Mauerbau. "Betriebskampfgruppen" versperren den Weg durch das Brandenburger Tor.
Construction of the Wall. The "workers' militias" block the way through the Brandenburg Gate.
Construction du Mur. Les "milices ouvrières" barrent la voie passant par la Porte de Brandebourg.

1945

Siegesparade der alliierten Streitkräfte auf der Charlottenburger Chaussee.
Victory Parade of the Allied Forces on Charlottenburger Chaussee.
Défilé de la victoire des Forces Alliées sur la Charlottenburger Chaussee.

1984

Parade der Schutzmächte auf der Straße des 17. Juni.
Parade of the Protecting Powers on the Strasse des 17. Juni.
Défilé des puissances de protection sur la Strasse des 17. Juni.

1948

Während der Berliner Blockade (Juni 1948 – Mai 1949) wird die Stadt durch die Luftbrücke versorgt.
During the Berlin Blockade (June 1948 – May 1949) the city received provisions through the Air Lift.
Pendant le Blocus de Berlin (juin 1948 – mai 1949) la ville est approvisionnée par le Pont aérien.

1990

Die Mauer ist 1989 gefallen. Der Grenzkontrollpunkt Checkpoint Charlie wird abgebaut.
The Wall fell in 1989. Checkpoint Charlie is dismantled.
Le Mur est tombé en 1989. Le Point de contrôle Checkpoint Charlie est démantelé.

13. On Safari

Sadly, or gladly? An end of an illustrious career with my Lancashire lads,
We start this short story with a new cap badge[1], beret, belt and future plans.
I will stay with my old regiment for the time being, whilst the new Corps forms,
And, as AGC(SPS), I am off to Kenya with the boys, I wonder how I will perform.

At 0400 hours on 12 October 1993, we sadly say goodbye to our loved ones,
The Advance Party[2] flies first and off to Tegel Airport, Berlin when the bus comes.
We are flying to Kenya via Riyadh, Saudi Arabia to refuel then off to Nairobi,
On landing at 2100 hours, Somalia is nearby, so we leave there with urgency[3].

An eternity flight behind us, we then drive up-country to the Nanyuki Showground,
We arrive there after 4 hours and for the next 8 weeks our home is this compound.
We are the Echelon[4] and we found our tent, got out our bags and slept somewhere,
After breakfast, we set up the base as per the plan, moving things here and there.

Nanyuki is a town in central Kenya and sits on the symbolic Equator,
With an altitude of 6389 feet and is known as the gateway to Mount Kenya.
This is where you see the famous marathon runners do their training,
We ran the same routes much slower and out of breath and they were singing.

The remainder of the regiment will be trickling in, in the next couple of days,
They will touch base with us then off onto the prairie in the hot dusty haze.
In October it can get hot and dry although it quickly transitions to wet,
The locals don't wear watches, they say it rains at midday like it is set.

The regiment will be making camp at Camp Masterson, at Archers Post,
The earned nickname of this place is otherwise known as Archers Roast.
It is home to the Samburu people and is over 100km from us at Nanyuki,
On the training area, commencing the anticipated, Exercise GRAND PRIX.

Exercise GRAND PRIX is one of the army's toughest training exercises,
It is one of the hottest places on the planet and you dread the sun rises.
It stretches soldiers to their limits in high temperatures with no escape,
Soldiers drill using live ammo in the world's most hospitable landscapes.

I was put in charge of the admin pool as my mentor had to stay behind,
It was very demanding and you don't get any thanks but I didn't mind.
Life can be a juggle in the jungle, I will make sure I enjoy my time here,
To Nanyuki once in a while and further afield to sample the local beer.

My job was to give admin and financial support and to help run the bar,
A busy day working in the office and often doing pay runs in the office car.
Paying dignitaries for use of the training area and buying supplies and rations,
Sometimes taking big bundles of cash by helicopter to various factions.

On time off, we walked out to Nanyuki and frequented the many pubs,
We probably paid extra for the beers outside especially in the clubs.
Tusker beer is the most popular, then Kenbrew and White Cap isn't bad,
Seeing the poor side of the shanty town and how the people live was sad.

We made a good deal with a local carpenter to make beds, say a score,
They cost a few pounds and when we leave, we will donate them to the poor.
I welcomed that comfy bed, especially when I was very ill and suffering,
I wrote a letter to my dad *just in case* but after a few days I was recovering.

We made a few day trips and long weekends to Aberdares and Elsamere,
Sweetwaters Camp to see the rhino up close and personal without fear.
A few days R&R[5] at the infamous Lake Naivasha, wildlife and afternoon tea,
The beautiful setting of Joy Adamson's book 'Born Free' a great true movie.

The Aberdare National Park is where a princess in February 1952 became queen,
We paused there for a moment standing exactly where The Queen had been.
With respect; Lee, myself, Nige and Mark were proud to be in that special place,
The road was blocked by elephants then scary ostriches were in the chase.

One of the things I would care to forget was when I fell into an ant's nest,
I was hurting, bitten which felt like burning and getting naked seemed best.
The lads helped me strip and I was covered in red blotches and bites presumably,
The coach full of tourists drove by and saw this white naked thing assumably.

The hippos swimming at Thompson's Falls was something to write home about,
The monkeys were a force to be reckoned with and pinch your stuff no doubt.
The very athletic chickens in the local restaurant were something of a bite,
The leanest chickens ever seen so eating a whole one only seemed right.

Kenyan delicacies in Nairobi on the other hand were something of a dish,
The RSM[6] insisted we sat on his table; I hope he is going to pay for the fish.
The next day, we had samosas for starters, followed by zebra steaks I think,
We had to try giraffe and buffalo meat but when they cooked it, it stinks.

Being out on safari proper, in the real wilderness of Kenya is a treat,
Zebras, giraffes and camels in their habitat and watching lions eating meat.
Our armed guard was welcome in some cases, now back to tents on sticks,
Why do the Gurkhas[7] put tabasco sauce on everything including Weetabix?

We left this spectacular country on 6 December 1993 to fly back to Germany,
Ending our 8 weeks in 'The Pearl of Africa' enroute to Berlin, I hope it is sunny.
Landing back at the very cold Tegel Airport and back to Barracks on the bus,
Driving home to the family and they commented on my tan and made a fuss.

---

[1] In 1992, the Adjutant General's Corps (AGC) was formed and approximately 1 year later, all Military Clerks would be asked to transfer over. I opted to transfer over to the AGC (Staff and Personal Support (SPS) Branch).
[2] The Advance Party—When a Regiment deploys somewhere, the departure order is; Advance Party and then the Main Bodies. There could also be a Pre-Advance Party.
[3] Nairobi Airport was being used for US and UN purposes because of the conflict in Somalia and we were not there for that. We were there a week after the Black Hawk Down Incident in the Battle of Mogadishu. We landed at a different part of the airport separate from the US and UN. We were in Kenya for completely different reasons, simply exercising and live-firing.
[4] Echelon—A military company/body of troops providing military support.
[5] R&R—Rest and Recuperation.
[6] RSM—Regimental Sergent Major.
[7] Gurkha—Gurkhas are soldiers from Nepal who are recruited into the British army, and have been for the last 200 years.

Mark and Neal, Nanyuki, Kenya. Nov 93.

Rhino time, Kenya. Nov 93.

14. Marathon Man

My first taste of distance running was probably running home from the farm,
In hindsight now, I am fully aware of how good it is to jog and it does you no harm.
Looking back to that time, I remember the 1-mile challenge and no not in a car,
In this case running down Walton Lane from the golf course to the Hour Glass bar.

Maybe I should have pursued distance running at school when I had the chance,
Wouldn't it be extremely handy if you could think of all of these things in advance.
But then, my life might have changed direction; would I have joined the army?
And, there is reality, I was not that good at distance running, quite average really.

So where did I get the 'buzz' for running long-distance? That is a good question,
The endurance and running the extra mile was the military training intervention.
Let's see where this running (and cycling) journey takes me, when did it start?
After a few years in the army, I can say being in the lead is as good as taking part.

My first half-marathon was probably a compulsory event for Regimental reasons,
We ran a half-marathon for Waterloo Day[1] but then we also ran in all seasons.
Two years later was a very proud voluntary running event; the 25km Berlin race,
The finish line was running into the Olympic Stadium and then upping the pace.

I was getting that 'buzz' for running, taking part in 10km cross-country races,
Running countless races over a 2-year period and finishing in good places.
Taking it seriously and stopping smoking on New Year's Eve to up my game,
Team champions and personally commended for the most races were my fame.

Training every Sunday was real commitment and I was now at my peak,
Enjoying the 6-pack on home videos, no not the beer kind, so to speak.
Half-marathon emotions saw me running the same race 3 times in 3 years,
1996 Cæsar's Run (half-marathon) and Brüggen[2] 10-mile road race saw tears.

Winners of the 10km cross-country championships 2000 was a great day,
The London marathon that same year saw me, John and Shirley on our way.
Driving from Gütersloh to the UK, then train to Newcastle return to London,
The husband-and-wife team lead the way and we all made it so job done.

London marathon was for donating, raising funds for a cerebral palsy charity,
Running for Rebekah, daughter of best friends Gary and Wendy gave me clarity.
Staying with them in Woolwich, a curry the night before and Bill was my aide,
In a huddle and sipping someone's beer along the way and the day was made.

Back living and working in my favourite city Berlin again was a busy time for me,
I tried my best to fulfil my hobby and made it to a Berliner cross-country meet.
I then trained hard for the Berlin marathon 2004 and running mate Vince pulled out,
On the day, I 'hit the wall'[3] early in the race but made it to the end and had no doubt.

Brüggen for another 10-mile road race but this time my running mate was my son,
Whilst I beat him on a street race prior, I knew he was fitter when we had begun.
He rightly beat me, I was so proud of him and then he was off to join the army,
But not before we cycled 200 km along the Mosel River, we must have been barmy.

The Köln Marathon in 2006 got away from me when I had to withdraw from it,
In training, I went over on my ankle and could no longer run, consequently unfit.
I had to have a ligament op which postponed my 'Down Under' plans for a year,
Final interview and was moving to Australia but changed my mind with a tear.

End of my serious running days with the exception of military training of course,
My second passion (and now my first) is cycling, a fitness activity I endorse.
Completing many River Mosel expeditions with my civilian colleagues was fun,
My target in 2022 was cycling the river alone and much further, another job done.

Cycling is an aerobic activity which is a good workout and gives you strength,
You get further, quicker and before you know it you have cycled some length.
Having cycled in Canada, Switzerland and Germany, especially the Mosel River,
Unable to run, or even walk far, then cycling is something you should consider.

Note from the poet:

After nearly 27 years of wearing army boots, military physical training and *voluntarily* taking part in the various marathon's etc. subsequently, I have had a difficult time in my later years, after having ankle, knee and two hip operations. Perhaps, had I done the minimum requirement (militarily) and not enjoyed running as my hobby, I would be much fitter today. I have absolutely no regrets with regards to my running days and wouldn't change a thing. Running is good for you; it gives you a real 'buzz'!

Event	Running/ Cycling	Dates and/or Year	Remarks
Adventure Training Canada (Cycling)	Cycling	1985	-Indirectly related to the serials below -Lake Louise-Radium Hot Springs -Approximately 130km (unsure time limit)
Waterloo Day Half-Marathon	Running	11 June 1992	1st Battalion The Queen's Lancashire Regiment (Berlin)
25km Berlin	Running	8 May 1994	Finish line in Olympic Stadium
10km cross-country races touring throughout British Forces Germany	Running	1994–1996	-Light Aid Detachment 1st Battalion Coldstream Guards Team -Minor Unit Champions 1996 -Completed countless races over a 2-year period -Personally commended for completing the most races in a year/season
REME Half-Marathon	Running	1994	Although I was Adjutant General Corps (AGC), I participated in the Royal Electrical and Mechanical Engineers (REME) Half-Marathon (special dispensation)

REME Half-Marathon	Running	1995	-Although I was Adjutant General Corps (AGC), I participated in the Royal Electrical and Mechanical Engineers (REME) Half-Marathon (special dispensation) *-Stopped smoking 31 December 1995*
REME Half-Marathon	Running	1996	Although I was Adjutant General Corps (AGC), I participated in the Royal Electrical and Mechanical Engineers (REME) Half-Marathon (special dispensation)
Cæsar's Run (Half-Marathon) Bracht, Germany	Running	10 March 1996	
Brüggen 10-Mile Road Race	Running	13 April 1996	*At my peak!*
100km Biel-Bienne International Run, Switzerland	Cycling (Support)	12–13 June 1998	-Support driver Bergen-Hohne to Switzerland -Support (cycle) for duration of overnight race
10km Cross-Country Championships	Running	2000	-1 General Support Regiment Royal Logistic Corps -Winners
London Marathon	Running	16 April 2000	-Final training run from Schloß Neuhaus to Oberntudorf, Germany (19km) -Travelled with John (colleague) and Shirley (BFBS) (Husband/Wife team), I ran alone. Gütersloh-London-Newcastle (collect Mum's husband Bill), London -Charity, donating money to The Bobath Centre (for Children with Cerebral Palsy). Running for Rebekah, daughter of best friends

			Stayed with Gary and Wendy in Woolwich for 2 days. Gary took us to the start point Blackheath, Greenwich Park
39. Berliner Cross-Country (8km)	Running	2002	
31. Berlin Marathon	Running	26 September 2004	-Final training run from Kaufland Dallgow-Döberitz (Havelpark) to Brandenburg Gate, Berlin, Germany (30km) -Not stopping when I passed my house -Matthew came with me on his bike
Brüggen 10-Mile Road Race	Running	8 April 2006	-With Matthew (son) (He beat me!)
Exercise MOSEL MARATHON	Cycling	2006	-55km approx. per day, 3 days -Military/Civilians (Joint Headquarters Rheindahlen Germany) -Along the Mosel River in Germany (Koblenz-Schweich)
Köln (Cologne) Marathon *(Withdrawn injured during training)*	Running	2006	-Operation on ankle -Application to join Australian Army/Move to Australia (having passed final interview/hurdle) postponed one year -Withdrew application to move to Australia (second thoughts and further discussions with family) *-Last running on this scale*
Exercise MOSEL MARATHON (self-named)	Cycling	2007	-200km over 3 days together with Matthew (son) -Along the Mosel River in Germany -Trier to Koblenz

Exercise MOSEL MARATHON	Cycling	14–17 June 2008	-55km approx. per day, 3 days -Military/civilians (Joint Headquarters Rheindahlen Germany) -Along the Mosel River in Germany (Koblenz-Schweich)
Exercise MOSEL MARATHON	Cycling	19–22 June 2009	-55km approx. per day, 3 days -Military/civilians (Joint Headquarters Rheindahlen Germany) -Along the Mosel River in Germany (Koblenz-Schweich)
Exercise MOSEL MARATHON	Cycling	25–28 June 2010	-50km approx. per day, 4 days -Military/civilians (Joint Headquarters Rheindahlen Germany) -Along the Mosel River in Germany (Trier to Koblenz)
Exercise MOSEL MARATHON (self-named)	Cycling	2022	-200km over 2 days, alone, e-bike -Along the Mosel River in Germany -Trier to Koblenz
Half-Marathon		21.0975 km	13.1094 miles
Marathon		42.195 km	26.2 miles

---

[1] Waterloo Day—The Battle of Waterloo was fought on Sunday 18th June 1815. A French army under the command of Napoleon was defeated. This Battle Honour/Special Day is celebrated by my Regiment.

[2] Brüggen—Municipality in North Rhine-Westphalia in Germany. The British military were based here, the barracks/airfield is where the race was conducted.

[3] Hitting the wall refers to the point in a race where your body simply runs out of energy.

LAD REME[1] Coldstream Guards Cross-Country Team 1996.

Neal London Marathon 2000.

Neal Berlin Marathon 2004.

My (Neal's) Major Running Medals.

---
[1] LAD REME – Light Aid Detachment, Royal Electrical Mechanical Engineers.

15. Being In/Complete

Summer 1995 and into autumn, and discussing that there was something missing,
Vanessa and Matthew out playing in the garden and we were broody and kissing.
Frank and family visiting and Marion and I were having a hot sizzling shower,
I apologised when I came downstairs for taking so long. Snap! I have the power.
Frank commented that it seemed we were only away for a few minutes, I laughed,
Making life is hard work sometimes and I reckon it took some real steamy graft.

Marion was feeling sick one morning and went to a local *lady*[1] doctor,
The doctor congratulated her with our pregnancy and it shocked her.
Celebrations were in hand but unfortunately Marion was not feeling very well,
One of the twins was lost and she must stay in bed for a couple of weeks, hell.
Cooped up in bed, twiddling her thumbs and phoning instructions downstairs,
Ordering daily Chinese takeaways and Gary, Wendy and all of us eating upstairs.

Christmas is now upon us and it is the only year that I am allowed to do the tree,
When Marion was up and about, she remarked that the tree was okay to a degree.
Grandma and Bill were visiting and then on New Year's Eve I gave up smoking,
I was in the middle of training hard with running competitions and was choking.
In a way, I thank this pregnancy as it gave me motivation and that extra drive,
No more stinky rollups and feeling very healthy, fit and winning runs with thrive.

Saturday 6th July 1996 started off as a normal day until Marion's water broke,
Do we have time to go shopping? After shopping she went to Claudia's, no joke.
She came home from Claudia and I told her off and took her to the hospital,
The hospital staff gave us a telling off and then I went back home for a little.
After pot noodles with the kids, I went back to the hospital and was told off again,
The midwife (Ruth) told me to stay put as the baby will be here shortly; when?

The baby is finally here and I told Marion we have a little girl, another daughter,
It took a while to revive Hannah and Marion asked for her and I brought her.
This little baby with her sort of blonde hair and the next day her hair was red,
Marion told the midwife that they had brought the wrong baby to her bed.

No, this little baby with the strawberry blonde hair is ours and ready for home,
The day we left hospital was freezing out so she was wrapped-up in her throne.

We were very protective of her, especially me but I was okay with that,
Meeting big sister and brother as she lies in her cradle in her little hat.
We were all besotted by her and I would sing many songs to her quietly,
The final piece of the puzzle is **complete** and we are now whole undeniably.
Before long we were packing and moving again and this time to Hohne,
I was off to Bosnia so I will have to endure her first Christmas without her.

In Hohne, in her door swing and making bubbles and family visiting,
Grandma and Bill, even Linda, Sara and Carl and times were riveting.
We went to many cool places and enjoyed going on our bike rides,
Hannah in her bike seat behind Mum, Vanessa, Matt and Dad guides.
She loved her carrots and it was no wonder she had an orange nose,
Tomatoes were exciting too, swirling her hands and twiddling her toes.

Almost 3 when we moved to Schloß Neuhaus and Daddy went away,
Daddy went to Kosovo but was back just before the Christmas Break.
Grandma and Bill enjoying Christmas with us, come on daddy Santa,
New Year's Eve Millennium fireworks and a very excited little Hannah.
Living close to our German family and often visiting Chocolate Oma,
Our German kin loved their English-speaking lot and me; beer with Opa.

Now 4-and-a-half and Dad's next job took us to Köln and very exciting,
Moving from a flat (with trouble no end) to a lovely house and no fighting.
Vanessa and Matt are off to St. Georges School[2], a short drive with Mum,
First impressions were joy and they know that they are going to have fun.
No army funding for Hannah to attend the school but Mum did a deal,
Mum worked in Reception Class and it paid Hannah's fees, what a steal.

Taking Hannah to a new friend's birthday party was a bit of a surprise,
Anke Engelke[3] was there with her daughter which was really quite nice.
Only 15 months in Köln and the job itself moved to Berlin, to the embassy,
Hannah now nearly 6 and ready for proper school and feeling very happy.
Hannah and her siblings all dressed the same and loving the uniformity,
Cambridge International School sounds prestige in Germany's capital city.

The kids came home from school without Hannah and then the hours were counted,
Hannah told the kids she was allowed to go to a birthday party and she was grounded.
Time to learn to ride her bike without stabilisers, so we drove off to the Havelpark,
Dropping Mum and Matt off halfway so they can rollerblade the rest of the part.
Dad teaching Hannah on the carpark, she was quick but not as fast as Vanessa,
And, by the time Mum and Matt arrived, Hannah was riding solo so there you are.

Matt would take her to the park around the corner from home and roleplay of sorts,
The kids loved being outside and if it wasn't cycling, it was playing other sports.
Winters in Berlin were white and along our road was Devil's Mountain to sledge a bit,
Translated from 'Teufelsberg' is not as scary as it sounds until you sledge down it.
So near to our home, this magnificent place, especially in the snow, you yearn,
That is, until you spend a lifetime climbing it to sledge down and crash and burn.

Vince was my equal Services colleague at work, his wife Tracy and daughter Katie,
New best friends Katie and Hannah went to a cancelled Westlife[4] concert, not happy.
The highlight was being a part of the British Embassy family, a chance of a lifetime,
Hannah went to work with Dad and sat in the office feeling important and sublime.
She saw our wonderful Queen and met the Duke and we had lunch with Jack Straw,
Of course, at only 8 years old she doesn't realise the significance of who she saw.

We welcome dippy Bonnie, a sister for Simba and Bes and poorly Bes passes away,
Who would realise what special kinship Bonnie and Hannah would have someday.
Holidaying at Lake Garda in Italy, driving through or overnighting in Ingolstadt,
The campsite was great, swimming with our caps and we had lots of fun and all that.
Visiting Sirmione's Scaliger Castle, Venice, Brescia and especially Verona obviously,
Specifically, Hannah loving visiting the setting of Romeo and Juliet notoriously.

Off to JHQ[5] for Dad's last job in the army and going off to St. Andrews School,
Dad coming home for lunch and Hannah would wave to me, she thought it was cool.
Loving the house across from her school and had a play room at home in the attic,
New friend Natalie and it was safe in the gated camp, in her element and ecstatic.
The camp was vast and like a town with shops, a swimming pool and a cinema,
Looking back on the Camcorder Classics and all them smiles, you should see her.

Hannah 11 and unfortunately has to reluctantly go to German High School in Erkelenz,
Dad left the army, staying in Germany and had to move from camp away from friends.
Part of life and it was hard, she only knew a little German but she never complained,

Keep the faith, she will pick up the language and can do this and she is determined.
Hannah meets her friend for life Dana who helps her and inseparable to present day,
Dad tips up with a kitten, Chummy, a little sister and new toy for the flock to play.

So, we jetted off to Egypt for 2 weeks; Mum, Dad, Hannah and Dana at 14,
Not there long and unfortunately our resort had a massive fire in-between.
Moving into a luxury hotel across the road and out walking which was lush,
Dad *had to* accompany the 3 sun-blonde and brown goddesses at a push.
Quad-trekking and Hannah went solo and we saw this figure in the distance,
Pillion it is then and back-ache next day saw the teens room-bound this once.

Whilst we were away in Egypt, Nadina and Leo volunteered to housesit,
Looking after the house and animals and obviously enjoying every bit.
We saw the photos and videos show of those two having a great time,
Nadina confidently driving Leo on excursions to Erkelenz sometimes.
When we got back, we gave them a treat and took them to Phantasialand,
We all had a great day out, especially Leo with his mum hand in hand.

Hannah changed high schools at 14 for her last 2 years and then her graduation,
Chummy had a hysterectomy and Hannah went with Dad for her reanimation.
Erkelenz Auditorium was her first haunt at sweet 16 until it sadly closed for good,
By midnight had she not got a note from her mum she had to be out of this hood.
I wonder who signed the note from Mum? Then off to the Diskothek at Himmerich,
Electrisize and other festivals, being part of the Karneval wagon is her granted wish.

Hannah is off to college for 2 years and summer 2012 we moved for the finality,
Dad and Hannah packed the barbie car with furniture for what seemed an eternity.
The final task was helping Dad with a wood-project, an impressive window sill,
All of this was done before Mum came home from work and she loves the sill still.
We had to keep a secret for her 18th birthday when Matt paid her a visit,
Driving all the way from the UK for her birthday and Hannah was in a crying fit.

A few gap months saw her at Kaufland[6] before starting her apprenticeship,
She chose hospitality with the Hilton Hotel for 3 years which sounds quite hip.
Dana started the course first and just like passing her driving test first, bless,
Something tells me that Hannah will start first elsewhere in life, a job no less.
Finishing her apprenticeship and shifts at the Hilton in Düsseldorf and much driving,
Driving from Erkelenz every day, often breaking down was upsetting and exhausting.

Holidaying for a week late autumn 2017 in Egypt with just Mum was good to see,
They even tried parasailing from a boat and they had fun bouncing in the sea.
Presented a better car for work and a former colleague is now her soulmate,
Promotions are not engaging her and Moritz and Hannah are out on many a date.
Hannah moves to Düsseldorf at 23 and Dad helps them out and she is very sad,
Sad because her dad didn't seem upset which Hannah thought was really bad.

Little does she know that Dad was indeed upset as he had an empty room to fill,
DVD shelves, desk, music centre and art stuff and somewhere for Dad to chill.
Off to the airport and Dad on a walking stick instead of crutches and unable to race,
Linda and Keith flew in from the UK for a long weekend and stayed at our place.
Feeling hip[7] and off to the shops in Holland and visiting Vanessa and her family,
The Chinese restaurant was dinner out and all of us had a fantastic time happily.

Not happy with her work and changing jobs is the answer and rediscovering that thirst,
Hannah content in her new job and Dana follows her, I told you Hann would be first.
Mum and Dad driving to Düsseldorf many times and especially on Hannah's Birthdays,
Meeting nearly all Moritz's family was nice and off to Duisburg Zoo, we had great days.
They now have kittens and her best friend Bonnie passes away which breaks her heart,
When Hannah lived at home, those two were as thick as thieves and never apart.

After 2 years at Düsseldorf, they decide to move back to much quieter Erkelenz,
Commuting every day is harder but at least she is near her parents and their friends.
One of the unsettled cats was rehoused and grand-cat Chewy is happier anyway,
Cat-sitting Chewy or sleepovers at grandparents when they want to go on holiday.
Moritz and Hannah very much in love and planning for a family and life isn't too bad,
Something we always cherish is the love and respect she has for her Mum and Dad.

P.S. Sorry for moving your room around, I was only trying to help!

---

[1] Gynaecologist.
[2] St. George's—The British International School Köln, Germany.
[3] Anke Engelke—Comedienne, actress, voice actress and television presenter.
[4] At least somebody turned up in Köln, Take That (even if it wasn't all of them).
[5] JHQ—Joint Headquarters, Mönchengladbach, Germany.
[6] Kaufland is a local supermarket
[7] Hip—It was shortly after a hip replacement operation.

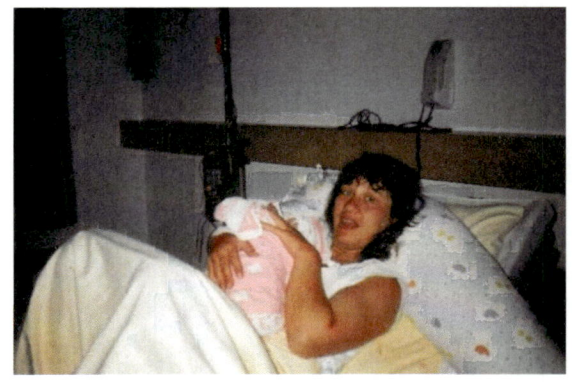

Marion (Mum) and baby Hannah July 1996.

Neal (Dad) and baby Hannah July 1996.

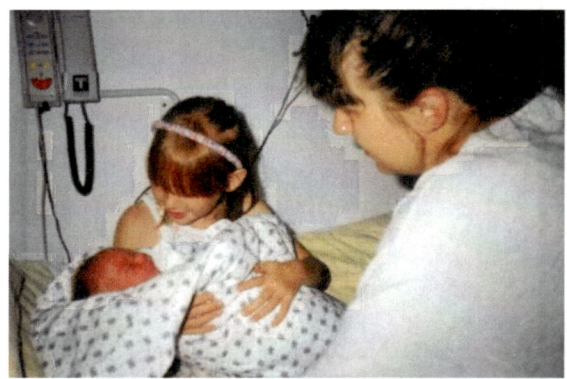

Marion (Mum), Vanessa and baby Hannah July 1996.

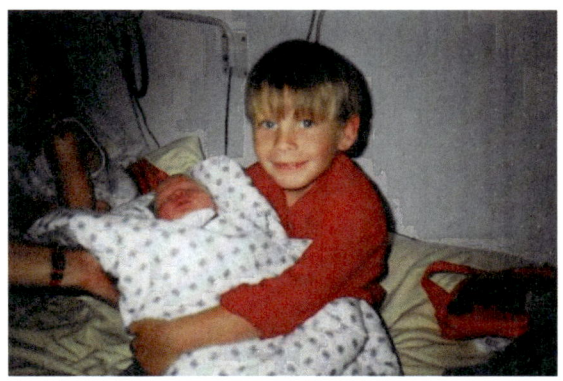

Matthew and baby Hannah July 1996.

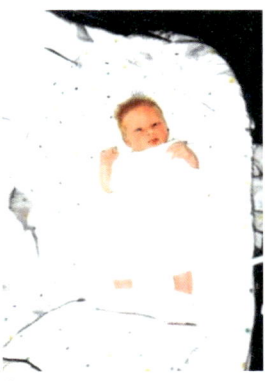

Baby Hannah.

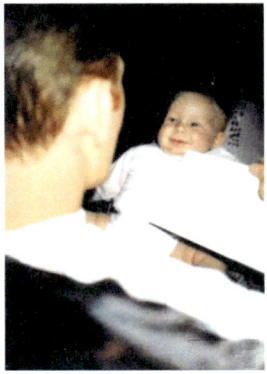

Neal (Dad) and baby Hannah 1996.

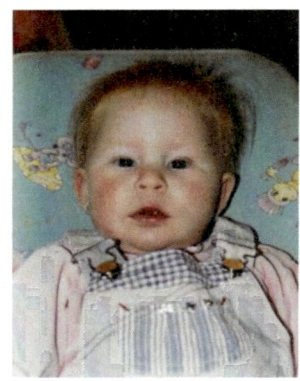

Baby Hannah.

Matthew and Hannah.

Vanessa and Hannah.

Hannah and Dana.

16. Balkans[1] Calling

Following the 1992–1995 war in Bosnia and Herzegovina, NATO played a key role,
Implementing the Dayton Peace Agreement through peacekeeping deployments control.
Over a nine-year period from December 1995 to December 2004 and as part of NATO,
I deployed to the Balkans with Engineers and then Logistics and my stories are below.

My first position as a new sergeant was, Chief Clerk for an Armoured Engineer Squadron,
Arriving at the base in Hohne[2], virtually empty as expected as the guys had already gone.
Just a couple of troops who were Rear Party[3] responsible for the welfare of our families,
Welcomed and proximately deployed from December 1996 to April 1997 as that's how it is.

I left my family and Germany just before Christmas and landed at Split Airport in Croatia,
I then warily travelled up-country approximately 200 kms to Mrkonjić Grad in Bosnia.
Our Base location was an unused Bus Depot and this was home for the next few months,
Supporting NATO on Operation RESOLUTE 3, in a Combat Engineer role on all fronts.

We were not there long when the NATO Operation changed name to LODESTAR 1,
From Implementation Force (IFOR) and the Stabilisation Force (SFOR) had begun.
Politics. The role of IFOR (Operation Joint Endeavour) was to implement the peace,
And, SFOR's role was to provide the stability necessary for consolidating the peace.

Mrkonjić Grad's elevation 591 metres, high in the mountains and my first recollection,
Was being snowed-in as we were involuntarily confined to our corimec[4] accommodation.
Meals were brought to us and passed through a window and the C.E.T.[5] dug us out,
Boxing Day all alone but at least the guys were using the tractor that had some clout.

Corimec neighbour Mick was in charge of the tractors and I was his new Chief Clerk,
So, at least we were one of the priorities to be dug out although it was almost dark.
Well, that was a long day so it was off to the bar to play cards, darts and pool,
Unfortunately, not much beer flowing though as we were on a strict two-can-rule.

Winter was hard, cold and curtains of falling snow was a typical day for the troops,
　Always out in the thick of it helping both military and civilians freed from the scoops.
　　I was responsible for all the administrative aspects and there were three staff,
　　　Me, another sergeant; Julie and our corporal; Nicky and we made it a laugh.

Receiving news was something we passed on when it is good news or even if it is bad,
　Important in the military family to come together and say a few words even when it is sad.
　　One of our colleagues from the same Corps as Julie, Nicky and I was tragically killed,
　　　Rest in peace 19-year-old Katy who was killed by helicopter rotor blades, it was feared.

It was certainly more pleasant when the snow cleared and we could get out of the base,
　We were out in the sticks and away from the centre of town and able to jog and race.
　　I recall a constant smell of burning wood and smoky chimneys, keeping the locals warm,
　　　Monday to Saturday was work and even most Sunday mornings too was the norm.

About halfway through the tour was our 2-weeks R&R[6], and a flight back to Germany,
A drive south and flight from Split to Hanover and a drive home to be with my family.
My youngest, Hannah, was only 5 months old when I left and we all had a lot of fun,
Vanessa, Matthew and my wife Marion glad to see me and a new routine[7] had begun.

One of the perks were the stays in Split camp next to the airport whilst waiting for flights,
Seeing a best friend Ricky, *although this was the last time I saw him*, was the highlight.
I swam in the Adriatic just to cross it off my list and drove the coast road somewhere,
Flurry of snow for the first time apparently and middle-aged ladies have dyed red hair.

I suppose one of the benefits of being there and far away from home were visitors,
　When VIP guests came all this way and in their own time to spend time with us.
Michael Portillo is a pleasant (all-smiles) fellow and always up for a laugh and a joke,
Champion boxer Frank Bruno autographed a message and photo for Marion, top bloke.

　Two years later, again as Chief Clerk I then deployed to Kosovo with a logistics unit,
First, I had to get them administratively ready for deployment as they were deemed unfit.
A pre-deployment inspection identified considerable administrative shortcomings,
This failure was not on my watch and 120 one-on-one dialogues with me is forthcoming.

Exercise ULAN EAGLE Drawsko Pomorskie Training Area, Poland for final training,
　A massive area outside the town of the same name, and why is it always raining?
　　There was trouble at home with an unruly family who were relocated which was bad,
　　　Hard for me so far from home but at least I was able to have words with the timid Dad.

Physically, mentally and administratively fit and now enroute to Pristina in Kosovo,
Walled by a steep mountain range makes landings and take-offs thrilling though.
Here we go, the anticipated Operation AGRICOLA II summer 1999 to the millennium,
I have no doubt that this operational tour will be nothing other than a condominium.

Whilst there is a significant amount of NATO troops based in Pristina, this is not for us,
We will be based just over the border in Macedonia[8] at Skopje Airport, a road trip by bus.
A couple of hours drive south and passed the vast wooden US Camp Bondsteel,
Their camp is 955 acres of land, a constructed *city* and the site and sight is unreal.

The US are always hard to beat whereas our location was mainly a corimec *town*,
Macedonia's capital's international airport in Petrovec with a runway view was sound.
Watching Air Force One with President Clinton land on my doorstep was a spectacle,
We were not allowed access to Bondsteel that day because of 'very important people.'

Watching the heaviest plane in the world land was the next highlight, it was gigantic,
Ukraine's famous Antonov is here and the boss rallied the squadron hierarchy for a pic.
Unfortunately, the photograph has been misplaced but it was a magnificent sight,
You could have probably posed the whole squadron in its mouth but it would be tight.

We had quite a selection based at our location, NATO's Forces from many lands,
I was the administration hub for most things so there was always a helping-hand.
The Special Forces never needed anything and the Canuck EME[9] were no bother,
Even Captain James Blunt passed through our offices for something or other.

The Canadian Armed Forces Engineers were based there to fix their helicopters,
It was quite a show, as once they were fixed it was test-flight time for the choppers.
Socialising with the Canucks and drinking our 'two beers,' they were a friendly bunch,
I wish my memorable test-flight chopper ride would have taken place before my lunch.

Like in Bosnia, we pretty much worked Monday to Saturday and sometimes Sunday,
Sunday mornings was voluntary welfare time with the younger ones followed by run day.
Sergeant Major Jeff was a top bloke and you couldn't refuse one of his runs, only short,
We measured out a 10km route over a mixed terrain and not so short or so we thought.

Home for R&R and on return, a trip 130 km southwest to Lake Ohrid[10] to decompress,
Overnighting in a lovely hotel at the lake and a nice telephone call home just to impress.
Sailing, swimming in the cold deep lake and jumping off sheer cliffs was breathtaking,
A fun-filled weekend with the guys and no combats and rifles and glad I was partaking.

A logistics-run and subsequent day out 220 km southeast to Greece's Thessaloniki port,
Business complete and a walk into the town to enjoy something normal of some sort.
Out on a duty-run elsewhere and visiting McDonald's in Skopje for lunch was a trifle,
It was a bad decision and there were consequences for being in there with a rifle.

Balkans Calling, subsequently 'Calling the Balkans' was a BFBS[11] initiative,
Linking serving men and women in the region with their families was imperative.
'Calling the Balkans' had a hugely positive impact—just as 'Family Favourites,'
Had done a half a century earlier. For us from Germany it proved massive hits.
So where did I fit in with this great initiative? I approached it in three ways:
The hub to aid with peripherals, know-how and my voluntary welfare days.
I took advantage on a personal level too so **I** could be linked to my family and friends,
Three-way explanation; **administrator**, **welfare** and for **personal** reasons.
Chief Clerk, was part of the welfare team in the squadron and the point of contact,
We had SSVC[12], BFBS, and the two British Forces newspapers in on the act.
For both of my deployments I made it my mission to embrace this initiative head-on,
We had video-calls direct with soldiers and their families and that was number one.
There were messages to and from soldiers and their families and dedications,
BFBS Sunday lunch played our favourite songs, lovely messages and celebrations.
Sixth Sense and Forces Weekly Echo newspapers are well and truly on board,
Writing messages and we even drew pictures to each other and we were never bored.
I volunteered to chair Sunday coffee mornings encouraging participation with the troops,
It proved very positive and I had a good few people of all ages in my meeting groups.
Here is a pen and paper and a dictionary and what is your and their favourite song?
Listen out on the radio or watch it on the TV and these sessions didn't take too long.
I too, took advantage in dedicating songs and the newspapers message chats,
It was so much fun, even talking, writing and drawing pictures in code and all that.
For a laugh, using nicknames and codes that only our circle was able to translate,
My family and friends group coordinating as UK and Germany collaborate.

P.S. Some soldiers simply do not like writing home as they think it is wuss,
Writing to Wifey, Hubby, Mum, Dad, their children and friends is too much fuss.
Then we have the faithful 'blueys'[13] which is mostly a free way to write home,
Receiving your 'bluey' from home is a good feeling and you don't feel alone.

I even 'lined' the 'blueys' to make it easy for them!

We were home just before Christmas and then the millennium celebrations,
My mum and her husband Bill also visited us and helped with the decorations.
Back to work and fearing the affected PCs where we had that *year 2000* notion,
For admirable work, this year is the year I am *selected for my next promotion.*

---

[1] Balkans—The Balkans corresponding partially with the Balkan Peninsula, is a geographical area in southeastern Europe with various geographical and historical definitions. The region takes its name from the Balkan Mountains that stretch throughout the whole of Bulgaria. The Balkan Peninsula is bordered by the Adriatic Sea in the Northwest, the Ionian Sea in the southwest, the Aegean Sea in the south, the Turkish straits in the east, and the Black Sea in the northeast. The northern border of the peninsula is variously defined. The highest point of the Balkans is Musal, 2,925 metres (9,596 ft), in the Rila mountain range, Bulgaria. The nature of this story/poem is to explain what I did in working with the North Atlantic Treaty Organisation (NATO) in the Balkans during the troubles in Bosnia and Herzegovina (supporting also from Croatia) and Kosovo (supporting also from Macedonia (North Macedonia as it is called today) and Greece in the mid-to-late 1990s.

[2] Hohne—Bergen-Hohne Garrison, Lüneburg Heath in the state of Lower Saxony in northern Germany. Next to the Bergen-Belsen Memorial from the former Prisoners of War (POW) concentration camp.

[3] Rear Party—Military personnel in the rear are usually called the rear detachment, and they are responsible for staffing, supplying and maintaining the rear elements. The rear is considered a crucial part of military organisation.

[4] Corimec—The Containerised Unit is the most common solution utilised as either living or office accommodation to be rapidly deployed in critical environments throughout the world. The units are supplied in a flat-pack configuration, including all prefabricated components and electrical system.

[5] C.E.T.—FV(Fighting Vehicle)180 Combat Engineer Tractor.

[6] R&R—Rest and Recuperation.

[7] Routine at home—You have to understand, our spouses have a good routine with the children and then the parent comes home and all that is changed and then changed again for the next stint and so on. The parent who is away should take this into consideration.

[8] Macedonia—Macedonia and Greece signed the Prespa Accord in June 2018 which, among other things, resolved the decades-long dispute over the Republic of Macedonia's name. In February 2019, Macedonia's name changed to the Republic of 'North Macedonia.'

[9] EME—Electrical and Mechanical Engineers (Canucks—Canadian).

[10] Lake Ohrid—is a lake which straddles the mountainous border between the southwestern part of North Macedonia and Eastern Albania. It is one of Europe's deepest and oldest lakes with a unique aquatic ecosystem of worldwide importance, with more than 200 endemic species.

[11] BFBS—British Forces Broadcasting Service.

[12] SSVC—Services Sound and Vision Corporation provides welfare entertainment and information to British service personnel and their families worldwide under the BFBS banner.

[13] Blueys—Forces Free Air Letters, also known as 'blueys,' are a way of sending letters and messages free to personnel deployed in certain locations.

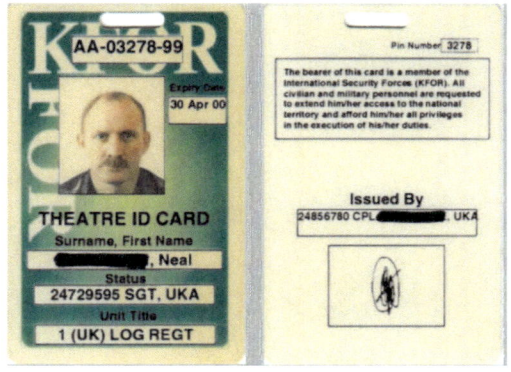

Neal KFOR ID.

With the lads at Lake Ohrid, Macedonia 1/5.

With the lads at Lake Ohrid, Macedonia 2/5.

With the lads at Lake Ohrid, Macedonia 3/5.

With the lads at Lake Ohrid, Macedonia 4/5.

With the lads at Lake Ohrid, Macedonia 5/5.

TEL: (0521) 924720   MIL TEL: Bielefeld 3482   FAX: (0521) 9247229   MIL FAX: Bielefeld 3483   SIXTH SENSE · DECEMBER 9, 1999

SIXTH SENSE

ADDRESS
Military
BFPO 39
Civil
Rochdale Kaserne
Oldentruperstr 65
33604 Bielefeld
TELEPHONE
From Germany
Civil: (0521) 924720
Mil: Bielefeld 3482
Civil Fax: (0521) 9247229
Mil Fax: Bielefeld 3483
From UK
Tel: 0049 521 924720
Fax: 0049 521 924722
E-mail:
sixth-sense@iok.net

EDITOR
Geraldine Dutton
DEPUTY EDITOR
Philip Welsh
ASSISTANT EDITOR
Ken Fish
CHIEF REPORTER
Jim Goff
FINANCIAL MANAGER
Melinda Jacobs
AD MANAGER
Sylvia Morgan
DEPUTY AD MANAGER
Vicky Wilson

Published weekly under the control of GOC UKSC (G) and exclusively for entitled members of BFG
Published for the British Forces Germany – raising money for charity.

DEADLINES
Advertising: Thursday noon
Cancellations 10 days prior to publishing date.
Page 2: Monday 9am
Letters: Friday 8.30am
Free ads: Thursday am
Editorial: Monday am

TECHNICAL SUPPORT
Tactica Solutions
Tel: 02161 551936

PRINTED BY
Verlagsgesellschaft Madsack GmbH, August-Madsack Strasse 1, 30559 Hannover 71

ANNOUNCEMENTS

BIRTHS

Det Hodkisson and Nina Siekmann: Would like to announce the birth of their son Liam Connor on November 20.

Ian and Alison Miley: Are proud to announce the safe arrival of their son Keir James, born on November 25.

BIRTHDAYS

Flt Lt Spike Wilson: A big happy birthday with love from all your girls Margaret, Kylie and Kitty. XXX

Chris: Happy birthday. Forever, Margaret. XXXX

Dad: Happy birthday – I can't believe anyone is that old!!! Love always, York and Vicky. XXX

To the loveliest Grandpa in the world – happy birthday – all my love, Kitty. xxx

Michael Tomlinson: Happy birthday pud! My little toyboy. Miss you loads, see you soon. Lots of love always, Vicky. XXX

Daddy Tomlinson: Happy 30th birthday, love and miss you loads. Lots of love and kisses. Ben and Abigail. XXXX

BIRTHDAYS

Jessica Hannah Cooper: Happy fifth birthday. Sorry I can't be there. Thinking of you always. Big hugs and kisses, Daddy.

Chris: Have a great birthday, I love and miss you loads. You mean the world to me. Lots of love, Rachel.

BECCY SAUNDERS
Happy birthday to you
Happy birthday to you
Happy birthday dear Beccy
Happy birthday to you

Hope you have a good one!

Love from Andy, Melinda and Sam. XXX

WELCOME HOME
Chris: Welcome to your new theatre!!! You will enjoy it here. Love, Chelle, Gemma, Charlie and Sarah.

LOVING
Man of the Match: Are you looking after my girls for me. Not long now, son. Make me proud, be good and keep smiling. Dad/Tippex loves you very much. XX

Ness/Hann: How are my little angels? I hope you are both being good. Hann will have to get out of Dad's bed soon! I love you, keep smiling, kisses, Dad. XX

Hi Baby Kirsten: Daddy here, to say that I love and miss you so much it hurts. Love, Daddy.

Sarah: Love you and miss you.
See you soon.
All my love,
Phil YYYY

LOVING

Jamie: Missing you darling. Days to do are still quite a few. Always your wife, lover and friend, Chris. XXX

Marion: Neal loves Marion because she's the strongest, most patient girl that he has ever known – he loves you. Love, Peggers

Mum: Welcome to Germany. It's lovely to see you and I've got loads of wine in ready! Love, Cleo. XXX

Ivan: Keep safe and maybe you'll get a Gameboy if you're really good! What do you think? Love, Cleo. XXXXX

Mr J: Home again, home again, jiggidy jig. Love you loads, Mrs J. XXX

Jackie Mitchell: Happy Christmas. We love you more than ten badgers and so does Daddy. We love you, Bethny and Elinor. XXX

Marty 'Muffin' Field: Always waiting for you. Love, your future wife.

Jackie: You're my type of bird because you stay in the kitchen and never say a word! D. XX

Jackie: Come up and see me (make me smile), I'll do what you want – running wild! D. XX

JR: Days to do are few they've said, put beer in the fridge and warm up the bed, all my love is always yours. Roscoe. XXXX

Beanie Baby: Love you more than words can ever say. You complete me, darling. Only 60ish days till you're back in my arms again and I can't wait. Love you

PERSONAL

Gloria and Ken: Great that you're over here for Christmas and New Year. Ken, the whiskey is on the bar. D Straker.

Please get well soon, we both need you and miss you. Lots of love, hugs 'n' stuff, Jason and Heather. XXXXX

Peggers: The love I have for you is growing each day. Not long to go before I have you in my arms again. I love you. Love, Moon. XX

Jullanne: Hi, my little angel, Daddy loves and misses you heaps. See you in January on R+R. Love and kisses always, Daddy.

Marie: Not long until the baby is born, keep your chin up R+R is coming. Love you loads, Mark.

Ed Palshiey: I've got 2000 Forecast Superbikes, so you'd better put a leave pass in now to the wife, Stan.

THANK YOU

Merry Christmas

Kim Nash and Pamela Thompson would like to thank all of the Garrison Volunteers for their invaluable support during 1999 and wish them a happy, peaceful Christmas and New Year.

LOST TOUCH

PENPALS

Pete Paradise, serving in Kosovo seeks letters and photos to warm up the year 2000. Write soon. Paradise Pete. Write to: BOX 4902, Sixth Sense, BFPO 39.

Single bored soldier in Kosovo, I'm over here for Christmas and New Year, wants young females to write to. Write to: BOX 4903, Sixth Sense, BFPO 39.

Firefighter in Kosovo, single, nickname of 'Cadders', wishes to hear from females who will light my fire over these dark winter nights. All letters answered. Write to: BOX 4904, Sixth Sense, BFPO 39.

LCpl D Spooner, 5ft 10in, black hair, blue eyes, looking for loads of mail over the millennium. Write to: BOX 4905, Sixth Sense, BFPO 39.

Soldier requires female penpals, any age, as long as you're good looking and game for a laugh. Write to: BOX 4906, Sixth Sense, BFPO 39.

I am female, 45-years-old, have two grown up children and three grandchildren. I am 5ft tall, medium build, have auburn hair and my eye colour changes

---

BULLETIN BOARD

To Val Rebecca Sam: Home Soon Love Dad Sorry Miss You Are XXXXX

To Kirsten: The love of my "LIFE" my darling wife. Love Linus X

Fussy Knickers: Keep Combing IT! Love always wide Boy

To R.E.M: I miss you more + more each day XXXX

TO DADDY I LOVE YOU LOVE T-C

Rondo: Love and miss you loads. Take care love always Denbe

To Cliff OO Victoria: Hi Beny, guess who? Chuntering the days till R+R, make you wife crusty. Don't forget I owe you a maybe 3, keep your fingers crossed. Love u Geruet

Victoria: You mean the world to me. I love you from the bottom of my heart. Thank you for every thing. Lots of love, Richard XXXXXXX

Happy Birthday Kay Clewett. Love You Babe, More Than Ever Love Fatboy XXX

HALLO BIG BEN: Many greetings from a white kitchen! Have a nice R+R Adventi-the 3 profit-dieson

LORNA: You make me so happy, love and miss you loads, see you soon Mxxx

To Steph + The Boys: I love + miss you all. Love Chris xxxx

MOON: To The Real Seal 2 RGJ R.E.M.E. Keep smiling don't let them get you down. Love D, L + R

To My Ice cube: Love and miss you more every day, can't wait for R+R love always Mo xxxx

TKH/DAD: Love you more than words, can't wait for R+R (car needs washing!!) Love + hugs Dawn Lee

Special Su: Thanks for making my birthday so great. I hope you enjoyed day Bossy. I'm unable to attend the second mass. Happy Thoughts

26 Regt R.A Kosovo: We've had loads of snow – very pretty – now we've got rain like the kings club looks grand. Now the Xmas decs are up. Keep shining. Love Aaarrgg-WRVS

My Darling Husband: B miss you very much. I hope you have a good Xmas and new year. See you and I love. Tenryo 18

NEW CANOE TIPEX!

TO SIMPS Love you forever Planks XXX

To My beautiful wife and sons: Love + miss you. See you Soon xx + x! mo! xx

My Precious Love and Missy Lexus, Really: Love you, more than anything can't wait to come home. Love + kisses Steve xxx

April, Abbey Asa, Missing: YOU ALL 3 1/2 weeks to go ALL MY LOVE ALB/Daddy

FAYE & SHELBY: See you soon Love Daddy X

Pegger 3: Keep your chin up! Love Moon

HONEY POT: I LOVE YOU SO MUCH SEE YOU VERY SOON LOVE HOT STICK

Lionel Bled 79 (Wilson): I am being good. Mummy is getting fat

Daddy: I am being good. Mummy is getting fat

SHELBY X FAYE SEE YOU SOON LOTS

All (Bunnies) The Davies + The Yanks: Have more fun Dan

BABES: HOPE THE FULL Lewish Murders are in the room when I get back

BROTHERS Now be nice

To Bedroom Bully: Love you loads. Miss you even more. Apples on the Frisbee moon.

BULLETIN BOARD

DISCLAIMER

The appearance of an advertisement in Sixth Sense does not constitute a seal of approval regarding the item or service advertised. Respondents to advertisements should take appropriate precautions before entering in to any contract.

Sixth Sense accepts no liability for any errors or omissions during production, including key codes, or the provision of proof copy before publication.

No other publication may reproduce any part of Sixth Sense, including articles and advertisements without the prior permission of the Editor.

Daisy Smith: Happy second birthday darling. Have a wonderful day and enjoy your party. All our love, Mummy, Daddy and Ellie.

Dee Magesan: GGGC. Happy 30th birthday sweetheart. Sorry I can't be with you. Have a good time in UK. All my love, John. XXX

Gary and Becky: Hope your day is good, b happy and full of pressies! We all miss The Bone Idles. Can't wait to see all of you. Lots of love and cuddles, Moon lover

Gemma Harper: Happy birthday. Four on October 18. Lots of love, Toby (our man). XXXX

8 years old October 16

Happy birthday to the best behaved, handsomest, politest, cleanest, hardest working and the most charming 8-year-old in our house!

Love from Mummy and Daddy

XXXXXXXX

12-years-old on Monday; October 11. Happy birthday, have a great day. Love, Mum and Dad. XXX

Faye Baker: Happy second birthday to our darling daughter, with lots of love and kisses, Mummy and Daddy. XXXXXXXX

Linda and Craig Wood: Love and miss you both loads, home soon. Take care, can't wait to see you again: Love Alan (Dad). XXX

Beanie Baby: Love you trillions and I'm missing you like crazy. Hurry home, Love, Joy Toy. XXX

Jamie Parrish: Your love has no missing parts. You're everything my heart desires. Miss you, love you more. Yours always, Sandra.

Sandra: I love and miss you loads, can't wait to get back and see you. Lots of love, Jamie (RS).

Dear Alan Love and miss you. Can't wait to see you, Love Ellie

To the best Daddy in the world. I love and miss you loads. Lots of kisses and hugs, Amy. XXXXX

Dear Alan No, nothing. Love Aimeé

Personal

Yo Tippy: 11 weeks to R+R. Can't wait to put my arms around you again. We all love and miss you very much. Lots of love and cuddles from Mom

BFPO 39.

Two lonely soldiers Bob and Mark, mad, outrageous, lonely lunatics seek similar female(s) for sparking a flame in a crazy postal party. If you fancy a giggle, give your pen a wiggle. Write to: BOX 4104, Sixth Sense, BFPO 39.

Hi, my name is Andy. I am a 20-year-old soldier. My interests are going down the gym, fishing and partying. I'm looking for someone to write to who knows how to enjoy themselves with a good sense of humour and time to write. Write to BOX 4105, Sixth Sense, BFPO 39.

Hiya Ladies! Two lads in Kosovo. Both desperately need stimulating mail. Don't be shy. Love Tony and Smudge. Write to BOX 4106, Sixth Sense, BFPO 39.

Sixth Sense is now online - Check it out now...
www.sixth-sense.co.uk

WIN DM50 CASH

FIND our Sixth Sense-reading bee (pictured right) who is hiding somewhere in this week's paper and you could win DM50 cash! Simply spot him and tell us on which page he is on. Send your entry to Spot the Bee 41, Sixth Sense, BFPO 39, to arrive not later than Wednesday, October 20. The first correct entry pulled out of the hat will receive the prize. All entries must be on an original coupon, cut from the Sixth Sense; no photocopies are allowed. The winner of Spot the Bee 39 (page 57) is M Taylor, BFPO 40.

SPOT THE SIXTH SENSE BEE

I have found the Sixth Sense-reading Bee on
page........
Name........
Address........

DEADLINE FOR Page 2 MESSAGES

PLEASE NOTE THAT THE DEADLINE FOR Page 2 MESSAGES IS 9am MONDAY.
MAKE SURE YOU POST BIRTHDAYS/ANNIVERSARIES ETC SO THAT THEY ARRIVE IN PLENTY OF TIME.

FREEPHONE HEALTHLINE
0800 1119652
FOR ALL ENQUIRIES ABOUT HEALTH AND THE BFG HEALTH SERVICE

Say it free in Sixth Sense

Announcements for marriages, birthdays, anniversaries, thank-yous, personal etc etc are all FREE in Sixth Sense, send them to: Announcements, Sixth Sense, BFPO 39.

Please fill in your name, address etc - not for publication

Name........
Address........

Tel no........
Signed........

Category:........
Date of birthday/anniversary:........

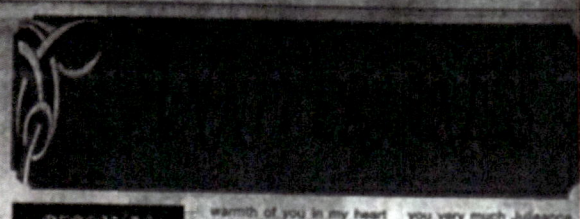

PERSONAL

TO JAMIE-LEE: Chris, Joshua and Gabby, I love you loads and can't wait to see you all in the New Year, take care of mummy, your loving daddy xxxx.

RENEE: We love you lots, you are the best mum in the world, keep smiling! Love Tracy, Michael and Mark.

MOON RIVER: Buzz Buzz it's me, nearly time to put the mobile away and give you some real buzzing romance, well we could get inbetween the sheets and also have a buzz, go on tell me to buzz off! Your proud little soldier Peggers!!

MATTHEW BROMLEY: I love and miss you more than anything in the world, where are my letters? Keep smiling babe, love Ulrika xxx.

SHARON PALMER: Can't believe you're back on the horse! Give the kids a kiss and a wet one for yourself, KP Nuts.

MUCKI: Not long now Honey Pot, can't wait to hold and kiss you, I am not going to let you go again, I will be yours always and forever, I love you and always will, love Peggers! Well done Matt for the football, hope Ness and Hann are being good for Mum, not long now Marion, days to do are getting few, we will soon be kissing and cuddling! Love you all.

MOON RIVER: Christmas is going to be very special, can't wait to wrap you up and then unwrap you, and just leave on your thong! Love you more than words can say, Peggers!

MY DARLING HERMIE: The nights are cold and lonely but having the warmth of you in my heart makes it bearable - just! Hurry home, always yours, Plug x.

BIRTHDAYS

PAUL HEMINGWAY (PJ): Just to wish you a great 5th birthday, love Steph, Steven, Jessie and Sam.

ELLEN AND CHRISTINA: Happy 14th and 10th birthdays, sorry that I cannot be there with you, Lesley I love you very much Julieanne, love and miss you, Jeff Daddy.

MATT BROMLEY: Happy birthday on the 15th, try to make it a special day, next year we'll celebrate together, love you always and forever, Ulrika.

EILEEN KEAN: Well blow me down, another year older and still no wiser, need a taxi, happy 50th birthday Grandma, love Gus, Jan, Lynsey and Stacey.

Echo Personals Every Week!!!

FREE Births, Anniversaries, Birthdays or other notices.

A free service to our readers.

We will be pleased to publish anniversaries, Birthdays and other items from our readers. Send details on this coupon, a postcard or in a letter to FORCES WEEKLY ECHO, PO Box 4, Farnborough, Hampshire, GU14 7LR, Great Britain. But remember that using the coupon will ensure prompt publication of your greeting.

Name.................................

Address...............................

ANNIVERSARIES

Keep in touch with your loved ones. Put a message in the Echo. It's **FREE** on this page.

CPL AND MRS DAY: Happy Anniversary to Scott and Emma, love from Mum and Dad Day. Hugs and kisses to Louise and Peter.
CPL AND MRS DAY: Very happy Anniversary to Scott and Emma, lots of love Grandma in Billingham.

LOVING ECHOES

DADDY (049): Can't wait to have you back so we can go swimming again and I can show you my 'loaties', lots of hugs and wet kisses from your favourite rugrat Callum.
CPL SAMBROOK: Sam I love you absolutely millions, I miss you so very much, thank you for a wonderful few days before you left, and thank you for being you, I love you baby, Les xxx.

BIRTHDAY

DARLING GABY B: Happy birthday, love and kisses Martin xxx.
MUMMY GABY B: Happy birthday, have a nice day, we love you, Jan and Luke xxx.
SAMANTHA WOOD: Happy 30th birthday, best wishes from all at 2Bn REME, BHQ, I hear Oil of Olay works wonders!
NICKY GILMORE: To my darling wife, happy 40th birthday, also lots of kisses from Matthew and Amy.
DALE PETER WHITE: Happy 1st birthday for the 21st Sept, sorry I can't be with you son, have a wonderful day, see you soon, love Daddy xxx.
DALE WHITE: Happy 1st birthday for the 21st Sept, love from Mammy and Daddy xxx. Happy birthday to the best brother Dale, only one year old, love from Paul and Andrew.

PERSONAL

'FAN BELTS': Biggest fan, I love you, I miss you, I got it do you want it, always yours, you know who.
LITTLE SMITH: Keep mummy warm and keep grinning, all my love Dad 049.
L/CPL PAUL STEWART: I love and miss you with all my heart, only 8 weeks to go until we are together again, love Leonora xxx.
TIGER: Absence really does make the heart grow fonder, what they don't say is how much it hurts! My ache is much better when I know how strong you are and you are strong, you make me very proud, I really do love and miss you very much Roar!
NESS: Matt and little Hannah, Dad is really proud that you are being good for mum, keep it up and maybe mum will take you on more day trips at the weekends, if you go to Hollywood Park again make sure the tigers stay off the car! Dad xxx.
TRACY 663: Days to do are getting few, can't wait to get back to you to be together with you is all I want, your love, as the nights pass I long to hold you tight and not let go, love Darren 663 xx.
BONE IDOL SMIFFO: Here we go again, miss you millions, what about visiting my lovely wife Moon River in Germany, I can arrange it! Wish you were here in this hot weather naked, well at least the Smiff wife, Tigtex.
HUGH: Can't wait to hold and kiss you on 13/10/99, missing you like crazy, love you honey, PD x.

THANKS

LINDA: Thank you for always supporting me through all the tours I've been away, the courses I've had to attend and the long exercises I've completed, but most of all my love, thank you for our two daughters Kerry and Faye, I love you, see you mid Oct, Steve xxx.

FREE Births, Anniversaries, Birthdays or other notices.

A free service to our readers.

We will be pleased to publish anniversaries, Birthdays and other items from our readers. Send details on this coupon, a postcard or in a letter to FORCES WEEKLY ECHO, PO Box 4, Farnborough, Hampshire, GU14 7LR, Great Britain. But remember that using the coupon will ensure prompt publication of your greeting.

Name ....
Address ....

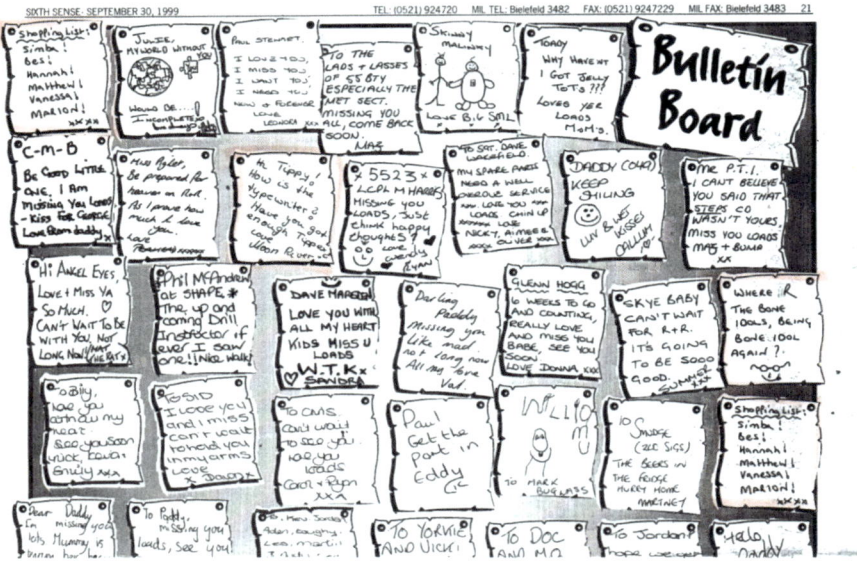

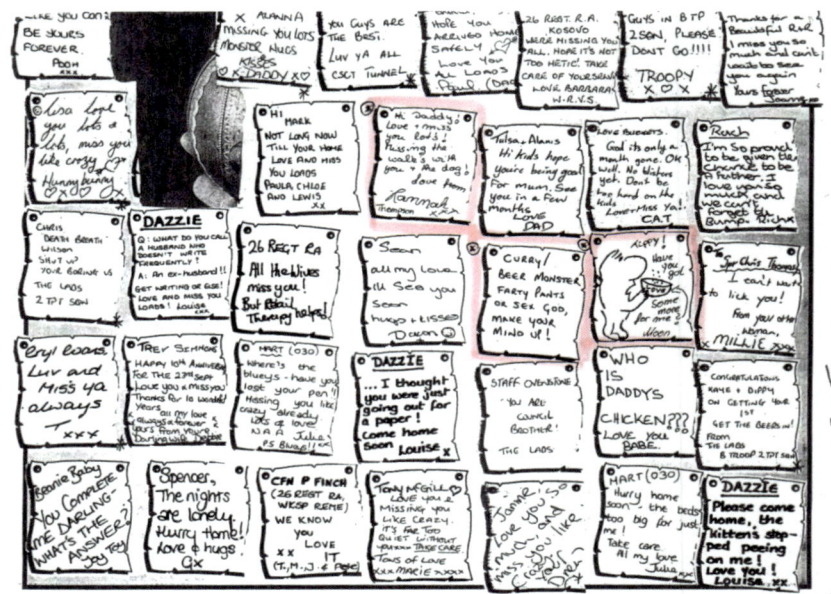

*The following two tributes were first written on the date stated (*) and were edited/extracted/slightly changed to poem (rhyme) format. They were letters to the family (with eulogy in mind). I have, where possible, **attempted** not to change them with the exception of perhaps the grammar. I have added more, but still relevant, content. I exclude full names to protect identities.*

I put this together on 17 November 2023, the date is exactly (to the day) between their two birthdays. *So, we have Ricky who died around 15th November 1997* and his heavenly birthday is 21st October and Keith who died around 8th October 2000* and his heavenly birthday is 15th December. We were all in the army and in the same regiment (before Ricky and I transferred and Keith was assigned to Special Duties). Ricky was still in the army when he died whereas Keith had recently left the army at the time he died.*

17. Lost Friends

Goodbye Ricky
First written 15 November 1997*

I have had the pleasure in knowing Ricky for the past 11 years (since 1986),
I was volunteered to be a clerk by the CSM[1], and then Ricky was in the mix.
Ricky took me under his wing and made life and work seem easy to enjoy,
From this day forward, my mentor was also a friend and one of the boys.

My most favourite memories were the nearly three years in Berlin 1992–94,
Friends, colleagues and even neighbours as he lived just metres from my door.
The neighbour's bit was convenient as we both liked each other's company,
Watching football together and the occasional Berliner Kindl bier or three.
Ricky sometimes helped me upstairs to my flat or I helped him downstairs,
The Everton and Liverpool fans occasionally woke for work a little unawares.
Drink-driving was never an issue although we admittedly flipped a coin,
To decide who would drive to work and who would be the one to appoint.
Ricky was right there when I was in Canada and my wife fell seriously ill,
He arranged for me to fly home immediately and the army to foot the bill.
When Ricky couldn't deploy to Kenya for a similar reason and me, already there,
I upped my game stepping into his role as well as mine so he could take care.

Attributable to being military administrators, we (voluntarily) transferred,
To AGC(SPS)[2] and posted away from our Regiment which we preferred.
Being away from the close-knit military family of the Lancashire lads,
Initially hard but promised each other to keep in touch and it wasn't too bad.
We telephoned each other once a month or so which generated a laugh,
Deployed on operations away from our families in the Balkans was naff.
The last time I saw Ricky in person was in February this year (1997),
Meeting in Split camp, Croatia and failing to get to our billets before 11.
We had one too many in the Sergeants' Mess and the camp RSM[3] was mad,
I was on a two-can rule up-country in Bosnia so being tanked-up was bad.
Ricky funnily mentioned, "Neal, you'll never change," but the question is,

"Who did I learn it from?" I replied, and that accountability was jokingly his.
Ricky's untimely death was wrong, it just isn't fair and his promotion,
And, preferred posting (reassignment) was imminently in motion.
He gave so much to the army and he only had a couple of years to do,
I know that Ricky and Wendy had many plans for their future too.
Especially that the boys were growing up and the thought of private-time,
Was something special to look forward to and somewhat so sublime.

Being regarded as one of Ricky's best friends is an honour,
And, I will cherish this respectful mindset forever.
A developed relationship from simply colleagues and mentor,
Neighbours and absolute best friends who naturally fitted together.
Ricky, a few years older and wiser and we had much in common,
And, his family; Wendy, William and Alexander will never be forgotten.
My loving thoughts are with them and I promise to keep in touch,
Relying on Ricky many times and it is his turn to rely on me as such.
It will be my pleasure to share gossip and the occasional social call,
Wendy and the boys are considered family and we will have a ball.

Ricky enjoyed his time at the UN in New York and his last role was undeniable,
Arranging the military administration aspects of Princess Diana's funeral.

I received a call from the Ministry of Defence confirming I was Ricky's friend,
He informed me of Ricky's untimely death and I was devastated no end.
I called Wendy to give her my love and condolences and to discuss his funeral,
She asked if I wanted to read a eulogy but I felt too junior to stand so tall.
We passed this honour to Lee who was somewhat more senior than me,
This poem (in normal format) was subsequently given to Wendy privately.
Travelling from Germany to Whitchurch, Shropshire on the overnight ferry,
Marion and I and the 3 children having fun and being (unintentionally) merry.
Dropping off the 3 children with different relatives and then driving away,
Overnighting at Wendy's and attending Ricky's Funeral was a very sad day.

Ricky was stationed in London and died from an aneurysm.

Sadly, we all lost real contact but I will never forget them.

Best Friend—Best Man
My Tribute to our Keith
First written on 8 October 2000*

The first time I had the pleasure in meeting Keith was on his first day in the battalion,
Joining the Queen's Lancashire Regiment who were based in Paderborn Garrison.
I had been in the Regiment over a year when Keith arrived at the Company Lines[4],
Having been there longer, I stepped in and welcomed him into our confines.
Keith and I became good friends from the offset, little did we know then,
That we would become this inseparable pair through thick and thin, amen.

A couple of things from the early days that stick in my mind; his 'greenness,'
After spending a substantial amount of money on surplus kit; that's 'keenness.'
The extra army kit and equipment which you would normally issue Special Forces,
Who were about to deploy on a patrol or an ambush which my point reinforces.
It made us both laugh when we joked about it, on the other hand, his enthusiasm,
The best soldier (me included), even in those early years, sheer professionalism.

I already trusted this man with my life!

Then came our first REAL[5] war when we were teamed up for an operational tour,
Off to Northern Ireland in our Brick[6]; Dougie, Steve, Keith and me, our Team of four.
There were incidents every day, soldiers were killed and severely wounded,
I can't write about everything now, therefore for this tribute, events are excluded.
In a nutshell, it was the most exciting but dangerous four months of our lives,
Luckily, our Brick and obviously most of us on this particular tour survives.
We constantly watched over one another and gave each other the protection,
Keith purposely went out of his way to ensure I remained focussed on reflection.
I admit that this younger man was a better soldier than I, he was my guardian angel,
A less experienced man saved my life at least once and brought me back from hell.

Something we should not probably admit is when I won those 2 concert tickets,
Madonna (*Who's That Girl* world tour) at Wembley Stadium and singing her hits.
Music was our thing for a long while, I had to endure his A-ha music non-stop,
Listening to music in his cars and making him listen to the king and queen of pop.

I love A-ha, I have all their albums and have seen them live in concert!

After Northern Ireland we got involved with two German girls, their practically sisters,
The girls later became our wives and then there were children to wonderful mothers.
We seemed to take after one another and the girls were soon in the family way,
We were both best man for each other's weddings on our very special days.
Our first children were born, Keith and Anka had David and we had Vanessa,
This history is set in stone and evidently, we will be best friends forever.
We were as thick as thieves and we had more children and more laughter,
Fun-times, separated sometimes but destined to be brother's hereafter.

Through change in time and service interest, we all sadly drifted apart,
Going our separate ways; Keith's time took him through a war and doing his part.
Keith, the soldier went to Bosnia and then onto other conflicts closer to home,
Neal the administrator saw a less exciting time transferring to another Corps alone.

Reassigned away from each other, my best friend, my best man!

Keeping in touch and did so but not as much as what we could or should have done,
We all say this when something happens but it is true, Keith was second to none.
What was nice, Nicky, an outstanding ex colleague of mine, put us back in touch,
Not believing it when she started to work with Keith and relating to the fate so much.
Had Keith and I met in person after so long, I am sure we would have embraced,
A man hug with my Best Friend, Best Man was overdue and then, a tragic waste.
A heart-wrenching accident took Keith away from us, such an untimely passing,
Keith and I and our wives and children were meant to be endlessly everlasting.

Keith had been through hell over his military years although he volunteered,
He relished in soldiering, especially the driving, a career which he steered.
I am certain he saved more lives than mine, that was how he was made,
He chose his own path in the army, a brave man who was never afraid.
Keith left the army earlier than expected to be with his loving family,
He yearned to be with them all and deserving to be together finally.
It was not Keith's time to leave us, this tragic death left families torn apart,
Anka, the children, his parents and his sister are now lives with broken hearts.

Anka, David and Kelly are not alone, they have lots of close and sincere friends,
Friends from our former Regiment who will be by their sides like their lives depend.
Anka and the children will be more united than ever now and even stronger,
I am sincerely sorry I could not make it to my best friend's funeral beside her.
I was holidaying abroad with my family and later respectfully visited his grave,
Anka and the children by our side as I said a few words, wishing he'd been saved.
Marion, Vanessa, Matthew and Hannah send their deepest sympathies to all of you,
If you do visit us as an angel, you would meet little Hannah for the first time too.
I told him that his family is forever in our hearts and that they can always rely on me,
Anka and the children were contemplating moving from Wigan and back to Germany.

I met his parents and his sister Julie a couple of times and this eulogy was for them,
Anka knows all of this content already, she knows all the tales and what we dreamt.

Keith was a Wigan fan in both football and rugby and his favourite German bier was Veltins. Anka and the children eventually returned to live here in Germany, her hometown (Paderborn).

Keith had left the army and was living in Wigan and died from his injuries from a road traffic accident (motorcycle/pillion passenger). His funeral procession was massive which included many military attendees including our old regiment and Special Forces personnel lining the street.

Sadly, we all lost real contact but I will never forget them.

Rest in peace.

Loyally Ricky and Keith Both Served.

*Closing note from the poet: Take a moment to think about the people you have lost over time. With the exception of family and other relations, I also lost other very sincere **friends and colleagues** and some of them are mentioned in this 'book of poems.' I am certain that I have forgotten some (and I apologise in advance for that). In no particular order, may you rest easy in grace and love; Arthur, Claudia, Martin, Jack, Nick, Derek, Billy, Tony, Jean, Lynn, Iain, Joe, Katy, (school pal Andrew who we had a very special lady in common who later gave him a wonderful daughter), Dave, Joe, Mark, Steve, Billy, Clive, Ned, Val, Steve, Cathy, Ron, Andre and Jürgen. RIP. Some names intentionally duplicated.*

[1] CSM—Company Sergeant Major, Warrant Officer Class Two.
[2] AGC(SPS)—Adjutant General's Corps (Staff and Personnel Support).
[3] RSM—Regimental Sergeant Major, Warrant Officer Class One.
[4] Company lines—Soldiers' accommodation.
[5] REAL War—Our Metaphor for the operational tour in Northern Ireland.
[6] Brick—An army patrol team of normally 4; point (person at the front), 2 in the middle and tail-end Charlie.

Ricky and Neal Berlin 1/2—11 Jun 92.

Ricky and Neal Berlin 2/2 11 Jun 92.

Keith and Neal at Keith's wedding Paderborn, Germany 1988.

Keith and Neal at Neal's wedding Paderborn, Germany 23 Dec 1988.

18. Day Trip to Egypt

Autumn 1998 my Engineer Squadron left for Exercise PINESTICK[1] in Cyprus[2],
I was left behind in my barracks squadron office in Germany, a sort of a plus.
Working on a project and when it was finished, I called my boss to let him know,
He told me to get my bones to Cyprus to *work?* And then a bit of a trip I undergo.

After flying to the UK, I then took a military flight to the Island of Aphrodite,
Landing in Akrotiri, a short road trip to Dhekelia and no Cyprus is not mighty.
It is only 100 kilometres north to south and 240 kilometres east to west,
Day-tripping to Larnaca, Nicosia and the untouched Famagusta was the best.

Famagusta, an untouched unfrightening ghost town made because of the troubles there,
The Turkish and Greek people were once at war and now have an island to share.
A motor glider flight was a highlight and viewing the beautiful sights from up above,
A drive to cold snowy Troodos[3] then we descend to a warm beach on this island of love.

Visiting tourists at Ayia Napa and then off to Cape Greco were more highlights,
How can this *work trip* get any better after taking in these wonderful sights?
Now fleeing off to Limassol with Gaz and Ned to catch a cruise ship to Egypt,
An overnight cruise to Egypt's Port Said and a coach trip to the pyramids.

If only I didn't eat too much at dinner and drank too many brandy sours,
Feeling sick as a dog and it seemed we were on the coach to Cairo for hours.
After a good 3 hours and arriving in Cairo where armed police guided traffic,
The Great Sphinx of Giza and the pyramid complex were very photogenic.

Like everyone, I thought the pyramids were in the middle of the desert,
This was my first (of many) trips to Egypt and in those days, I was no expert.
Giza is an Egyptian city on the west bank of the Nile, near to Cairo,
Crossing the bridge over the Nile River was also spectacular you know.

The Giza Plateau is a place to visit and I have also visited this place since,
These ancient Egyptian monuments stand to commemorate many a prince.
Life after death is glorified as death was seen as merely the beginning,
The beginning of another journey to the other world and it was mesmerising.

Going inside the Great Pyramid was claustrophobic in the very little open space,
Hunching through the passage sluggishly between tourists but keeping pace.
A passage with ascending and descending branches upward and downward,
The descending branch leads to the underground chamber we had conquered.

For some reason, exiting the pyramid was much quicker as we hunched to the light,
The cooler musty air behind us as we breathed the warm air and the sky was bright.
A short walk to the Great Sphinx donning our haggled fezzes for a photo opportunity,
Negotiating the locals to the coach bound for the Egyptian Museum in the capital city.

In Cairo, Egypt for just the day and back to the MS Princesa Marissa cruise ship,
This magnificent excursion to Egypt for the first time of many was a fantastic trip.
Revisiting 20 years later, this fez-donning belly-dancing poet and his lovely wife,
Flying to Cairo for the day visiting Giza and also cruising the Nile, oh what a life.

---

[1] Exercise PINESTICK is a regular deployment by a Royal Engineer squadron to build and renovate infrastructure used by British military personnel based on the island and the wider Cypriot community.

[2] The British Armed Forces are permanently based in Cyprus (Sovereign Base Areas are Akrotiri and Dhekelia) and troops and families are located mainly at; Akrotiri, Dhekelia, Episkopi, Limassol and Nicosia.

[3] Troodos Mountains of Cyprus, Mt Olympus, or Chionistra, at 1,952 metres, is the highest point in Cyprus.

Neal at Cape Greco Cyprus Nov 98.

Neal Motor Glider Cyprus Nov 98.

Gaz, Ned and Neal on board MS Princesa Marissa Nov 98.

Neal, Ned and Gaz Giza Plateau Egypt Nov 98.

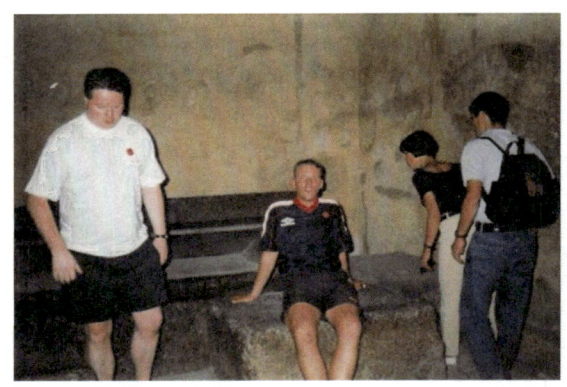

Gaz inside the Pyramid chamber Nov 98.

Neal inside the Pyramid chamber Nov 98.

Ned inside the Pyramid passage Nov 98.

Gaz and Ned at the Egyptian Museum Cairo Nov 98.

Neal and Marion at the pyramids Jan 2019.

Neal and Marion at the Great Sphinx Jan 2019.

19. Köln
(German, Cologne in English)

It is Monday 11 September 2023; 22 years ago today, we lived in Cologne[1],
I was always writing this poem; it is on my list and how time has flown.
It seemed fitting to write the poem today, I was simply compelled to do so,
It will take me a couple of days to write, but at least I started it today you know.

I have always related Cologne[2] to the September 11 attacks which I will explain,
I had been living and working in Cologne for 9 months when we all felt this pain.
As part of my job, I was co-located with my American military counterparts,
They had family and friends living in the Manhattan area and were in our hearts.

New Year 2001, my family and I moved to Cologne, I felt privileged and guilty[3],
I wasn't sure at the time, how long we would be living in this magnificent city.
For a British soldier to be posted[4] here was extremely unusual and unheard of,
Nevertheless, we are here now, making a visit to the Dom Platz and looking above.

When on the Dom Platz and you look skywards, you are amazed at what you see,
157 metres, the cathedral is the tallest twin-spired church in the world and entry is free.
Cologne Cathedral is Germany's most visited landmark; 20,000 people visit per day,
The police are friendly with us and the tourists and my children are inline skating away.

After World War 2 there were British military based near Cologne until the nineties,
The British Forces Broadcasting Services[5] were located in Cologne until the eighties.
The closed BFBS Studio in Cologne is literally down the street from where we live,
It is so sad to see this place so desolate, a waste, as this place had so much to give.

There were not many Brits here now, just me and my colonels working in Cologne,
And, a couple of senior military officers and civilians that worked in nearby Bonn.
They worked at the German Ministry of Defence in Bonn and we worked right here,
The colonels and I worked literally across the road at the Heeresamt[6], it was premier.

My job was support staff for the British Army Liaison Organisation[7] across Germany,
On my first day in office, I was told the job was moving to Berlin, into the embassy.
We would be here for only 15 months but we will thoroughly embrace the time however,
A very unique place to live and work with families joining in social events together.

We had liaison officers throughout Germany which needed my support,
That support would require me to visit them personally and make a report.
Fly, drive or travel by train across Germany; north, east, south and west,
As far north as Hamburg, south as Munich and even Berlin in the east.

It was an exclusive place to live and they were filming drama on our street,
Taking the dog out for a walk and then watching the police cars screech.
I thought it was real at first and there were bad words painted on a house,
The camera crew and police were laughing and joking and a fire was doused.

Our children were enrolled at St. Georges British International School,
An exclusive school in Cologne and TV personalities children are there too.
The army paid our school fees but unfortunately not for our youngest one,
So, her mum got a job with reception class which paid the fees, so job done.

Living a couple of hundred metres away from the river Rhine was bliss,
Walking, running and cycling along the river and watching the ships.
Getting in and out of Cologne was a problem though; traffic congestion,
Staying home, especially in winter would have been a good suggestion.

Tuesday 11 September 2001 was a normal day in the office as it often is,
My colonels were away on business and I was alone manning the offices.
The senior colonel called me and asked if I had seen the news on the television,
I put on the television and watched in horror; it must have been terrorism?

The senior colonel told me to visit the US office to see if they had heard the news,
I ran to their office and saw the shock in other offices and hearing their views.
The US Colonel and Major were buried in the news and watching with disbelief,
The Major was crying and trying to call his family in New York so my visit was brief.

I called home and my wife was watching it on the news, a very sad day,
She went to collect the children from school and saw sadness along the way.
The school, streets, neighbourhood and the whole city were in total shock,
America was under attack; we are all under attack and we were taking stock.

Next day, our German General called a parade, rows and columns of solemn faces,
The whole of Germany's military was sombrely commemorating in their bases.
All flags are at half-mast and we encircled our US colleagues with compassion,
This tragedy will not go unpunished and the US and its Allies will take action.

1st March 2002, another sad day for some when the Deutsch Mark was no more,
The €uro was the currency now and something to get used to, now that it is law.
The funny thing is, that today, we are still comparing the prices and converting,
We have definitely lost out which we had to live with and it is very frustrating.

British Army Liaison Organisation (Germany) (BLO (Ge)):

BLO	Location	Remarks/MoT[8]
Senior Officer (Colonel)	Cologne	Plus myself (I was the Staff Assistant)
Force Development (Lt Col)	*Cologne*	*Once the senior officer and I moved to Berlin**
(Academy) (Lt Col)	Hamburg	(German equivalent of Sandhurst[9])/Fly
ENTEC[10] (Lt Col)	Munich	Train
German Army Forces Command	Koblenz	Drive (Fly when from Berlin)
Logistics (Lt Col[11])	Cologne	Co-located
Artillery (Lt Col)	Idar-Oberstein[12]	Drive
Armoured (Lt Col)	Munster (Örtze)	Fly and Drive
Infantry (Lt Col)	Hammelburg	Drive

*I did not return to the Heeresamt once I moved to Berlin, it was deemed unnecessary.

No names are mentioned in this poem to protect identities.

[1] Cologne—Köln, Germany.
[2] My time in Cologne.
[3] Guilty—'nice guilty' if that makes sense.
[4] Posted—A military term, to be assigned somewhere, move jobs and family.
[5] British Forces Broadcasting Service (BFBS)—Provides TV, live sports, radio, cinema, news, live events and much more for the HM British Forces and their families all over the world.
[6] Heeresamt—German Army Office, Cologne.
[7] British Army Liaison Organisation (Germany)—BLO (Ge). British Liaison Officer (BLO).
[8] Method of Travel (preferred) (and only if required).
[9] The German Officer's Academy, the equivalent of Sandhurst in the UK.
[10] ENTEC—German Military Engineering Centre of Excellence.
[11] Lt Col—Lieutenant Colonel.
[12] FYI—Bruce Willis was born here.

Hannah in Cologne 2001.

Matthew and Hannah in Cologne 2001.

Neal's family in Cologne 2001.

20. Highpoint

Berlin 2[1]:

Yes, my dear, my job here is moving to Berlin, to the embassy, you see,
Packing in Cologne, and the family saying "see you soon" to me.
I move first, to take over our new home and the office, this is all for us,
And seeing the embassy for the first time, the structure is flawless.

British Embassy Berlin:

The architecture is purely majestic and I felt truly honoured,
The sandstone frontage is stately and I stayed there and pondered.
The entry to the courtyard with its oak tree which symbolises Britain,
The grand staircase leads to where I wonder and I am smitten.

The climb up the stairs is a sight on its own and voices sounded,
The vertical void space is immense and the auditorium is rounded.
The banqueting hall and winter garden exhibit several works of art,
The views left, right, above and below are simply worlds apart.

The coloured auditorium and projecting library are seen from the street,
The inside area adjacent to these rooms is where we meet and greet.
The library translucent windows offer a great view of the outside,
The walkways above the hall offer abundant views of the inside.

Work:

Swiftly settling in, I am not here to defend it, but to represent it,
Sometimes in uniform but most times in a suit and tie, a good fit.
Our tri-service section and support staff share many points of view,
Diplomats, foreign dignitaries and politicians are two a penny too.

The team then; Attachés Brigadier 'Rob' and Colonel's 'Jack' then 'Mike,'
Colonel 'Jack' had been a boss of mine for a long time[2], there and back.
All of our wives, Mick (and Lisa) and Vince are my equal of course,
Nick, Gayle and Charleen and the other Attachés; Navy and Airforce.

My day was never the same and sometimes I am required elsewhere,
Travelling across Germany visiting our army liaison team there.
Meeting VIPs is also part of my day and wow… Prince Charles is here,
Neglecting etiquette, I met him out of uniform and broke protocol, I fear.

Now, Robbie Williams is gracing us with his presence, 'take that,'
Promoting a solo album and on the galleries above, we quietly sat.
Then, shouting from the terraces "come on Blackpool, come on Burnley,"
He responds looking up, smiles and returns "come on Port Vale" with glee.

The Main Highlight:

State Visit of Her Majesty the Queen and the Duke of Edinburgh is here,
Responsibilities and wearing best uniforms for the highlight of the year.
Our first task is the royals' visit to a famous graveyard in Berlin's east,
Then the evening invitation and the royals meet our families at the feast.

The gala concert is the next serial and wearing Mess Dress feels fitting and nice,
Personally, escorting the royal pair and ensuring the coordination is precise.
Obliviously, speaking to Her Majesty when I shouldn't, wasn't part of my plan,
The Queen rightly ignored me as she knew it was a mistake, I am but a man.

Receiving personal thanks from my British ambassadors in my time 2002–2005,
Namely Sir Paul Lever and Sir Peter Torry for a job well done, I am gratified.

Fond Farewell:

I remember my last day very clearly, 7/7 (2005), the London bombings,
I was saying farewell to colleagues, and some were sadly sobbing.
Nevertheless, I wasn't going to let terrorists spoil my time there,
Time at the embassy was the highpoint of my life and something to share.

[1] The second time I was posted to Berlin, the first time was in 1992.
[2] Colonel Jack (his Christian name) was first my Officer Commanding in Paderborn, Germany as a Major, then Lieutenant Colonel when he was my Commanding Officer in York, UK and at this time, my Colonel, Military Attaché British Embassy Berlin/Senior British Liaison Officer (Germany).

HRH State Visit to Germany Nov 2004, at Stahnsdorf Cemetery nr Berlin. Neal at the rear.

Neal with Col 'Mike' at Brandenburg Gate commemorating World War II, May 2005.

21. Adult Education

Well, how do you write a poem about Adult Education and why would you?
Having left school with very little to nothing, it is something important to do.
In hindsight, having achieved what I have over my adult years, I know now,
I can read and write well and if you were here, I would rightly show you how.
I should have and could have done better at school and think it was defiance,
Maybe I rebelled, blame my upbringing or simply didn't support compliance.
A big mistake on my part and for that I am sorry; apologising to my teachers,
Just sat there, stubborn and not interested and not letting them reach us.
Leaving school just short of 16 and not really knowing what I was going to do,
Something had to give and at 19, I would finally *find my way* as only I knew.

I join the army and if I am honest, I think, how the hell can they educate me?
Let's start with the first day or week or so and they will surely make me see.
Identifying early on that I didn't leave school with much placed me as special,
I would always be made to sit at the front of the classes which I found typical.
Obviously, I could read and write and there were recruits worse off than me,
I found myself eagerly learning and even helping others as we are a team.
Just over the 5-month basic training showed me the way of the importance,
Fitness and shooting as well as good education equal an overall performance.
Reading and writing various military reports and reading maps and on the ranges,
English, geography and mathematics for shooting as the wind involves changes.

So that is basic education out of the way and off to your regiment somewhere,
In my case, off to Germany, the first time abroad and speaking German there.
Ironic really, as my dear old German teacher at school tried her absolute best,
I had zero interest, bless her and now I will be involuntarily put to the test.
Introduction to German quickly followed by basic German was an obligation,
Eventually finding my ideal army trade finds me working in administration.
Marrying my German girlfriend and starting a family and living in Germany,
Now 23, a sensible married man, a little better educated and living in harmony.
Administration qualifications were building up and looking forward to promotion,
Being promoted in the army requires a certain amount of military education.

You can feel where I am going with this, over time, I am being better educated,
Living mostly in Germany and earning promotion means you have been dedicated.
More German language qualifications follow as well as a trade class upgrade,
Promoted from Lance Corporal to Corporal and now a Sergeant, I was made.
Just over 30, it has been 14 years since leaving school and things are looking good,
An educated soldier who is very good at his job and no more kid from the hood.
Things can only get better as we transform from forms and files to a computer,
Computers have been on our desks but are now the fighting force of the future.
It is only fitting that a sergeant administrator gets on board with the learning,
German language is improving and computer qualifications are worth yearning.

Adult Education is well and truly part of my life as it is never too late to learn,
Working hard at bettering yourself and promotion is something you have to earn.
All of the above has paid off and this new staff sergeant is off to pastures new,
I am now sat in a British Military Liaison Office in a German Army Headquarters too.
Luckily, with German language under my belt, I was selected for the embassy,
This prize is something you only read about as I am off to Germany's capital city.
This prestigious British Embassy post will become the *highpoint* of my career,
Looking back at my past 16 years, I realise it is the education that got me here.
It was here in Berlin that I had to go away for a 4-week promotion military education,
Educationally qualifying to become a Warrant Officer Class Two was the realisation.

Like everything else education, I find it very hard and definitely a personal test,
After extra revision, gaining qualifications in English and Maths from doing my best.
Working with the Queen and the Duke on their State Visit to Germany is behind me,
No, it really does not get better than that but now I have another good opportunity.
Realistically, I was going on my last assignment before retiring from the army,
Also, resettling and allowed to work on further education which is good for me.
Now 40+ and still eager to learn and it was at this time when I earned more awards,
For previous qualifications, the embassy work and recommendations towards.
I was gratefully awarded the International Diploma in Administrative Management,
I was also awarded City and Guilds Awards for English and Maths for work spent.

My expected retirement saw me earning more qualifications I could use to resettle,
Office work, health and safety and more computer qualifications to help me settle.
Had I retired to the UK, I could have undoubtedly landed a good managerial position,
But we chose to stay in Germany and it is going to be hard but this is our decision.
Finding my feet for a couple of months and then came a phone call from the military,

"Would I like to return to JHQ[1] as a full-time reservist?" And said "yes" immediately.
Attributable to who I am and what I had accomplished, they made a position for me,
My education as well as qualifications and experience gave me this unique opportunity.
Retirement on hold for a few years and now working in media and communications,
This office manager is off to the UK to train as a military journalist in public relations.

Practically immediately promoted to Warrant Officer Class Two as I was ready,
I had run out of time on my first time round but now my military time is steady.
At this stage in my life, about 45 and very much in full swing of learning and training,
I admit that it has all been very hard, as I am not a brain box and it can be draining.
Thinking back to school where there was no one there to give me the push I needed,
My circle of friends and colleagues both military and civil servants who I heeded.
Haley, Dave, Nikki, Gareth, Debbie, Peter, Becky, Rab, Ren and Phil gave me the edge,
Their individual encouragement was second to none and for that I gave my pledge.
I managed to obtain more computer qualifications as you do just because I can,
The unqualified teenager who found his way had become a very well-educated man.

Summoned to the UK for interview, well, asked if I wanted my job 'as a civil servant,'
I said "yes," but time later, there was a massive change in the UK government.
British Forces Germany was drawing down and unfortunately my job was lost,
This is it now, I am finally leaving the army 'proper' as my 'top job' was quashed.
I'd had a good run and after nearly 27 years in the military, I am hesitantly retiring,
I decided to take a year out and then I had that craving again, to feel inspiring.
At 48, I went back to school, German night school, to learn a higher level of German,
After 3-months I earned a diploma and enough to become a naturalised German.
I didn't take the nationality and remain in Germany as a resident which is okay,
Another entry in my CV and after an interview, I landed a good job; "hear, hear," I say.

Training/Qualification	Date/Age (years)	Remarks
Introduction to German Language	200588 (almost 23 yrs.)	
Army Clerical Administrator Class 2	201188–091288 (23 yrs.)	Army Trade Qualification
Basic German	20–300689 (24 yrs.)	Grade C
Colloquial German Test	011289 (24 yrs.)	German Level 2 (Survival) equivalent A-Level
Army Clerical Administrator Class 1	10–230690 (25 yrs.)	Army Trade Qualification
Unit Documentation Course	08–121090 (25 yrs.)	Army Clerical Administrator Specialist Qualification—Grade B
Education Promotion Certificate	Approx. 300691–300791 (26 yrs.)	**Educationally Qualified to become a Sergeant:** Communication Skills (English equivalent A-Level) Military Calculations (Mathematics equivalent A-Level) Military Management
Advanced Word Perfect	18–190794 (29 yrs.)	Computer Studies prior to Microsoft
German/English Partnership Seminar	08–120500 (35 yrs.)	Strausberg. No qualification (Military—selected to participate)
Selected for British Embassy Berlin	03/2002	Exempt Long German Course
Education for Promotion Scheme Level Two	Approx. 040503–040603 (38 yrs.)	**Educationally Qualified to become a Warrant Officer Class Two:** *Army Defence Studies/Military Management Studies:*

		Current Issues Defence Missions and Tasks—Grade C
Current Affairs British Defence Policy—Grade C
Principles Processes Management Military Organisations—Grade C
Effectiveness Management Systems Proposition Strategies Improvement—Grade C
Identification Extraction Relevant Information Solve Problems—Grade B
English (Diploma) (Military Specialism in mind)—Grade B
Communication Complex Information Ideas Discussions Briefings Presentations—Grade C, this subject couples with English (Diploma) above
Application Numerical Date Support Decision Making (Mathematics (Diploma))—Grade C
Warrant Officer's Command, Leadership and Management (Part 2)	16–200804 (39 yrs.)	Command, Leadership, Standards and Discipline, Advise and Guide Subordinates, Communications (Written and Oral), Routine Military Duties and Manage Personnel Administration (*Green-Competent*)
City and Guilds Communication Sills Level III	02/2005 (almost 40 yrs.)	English Award
City and Guilds Numeracy Stage 2	04/2005 (almost 40 yrs.)	Mathematics Award
Member of the Institute for Assistants to International Military Attachés Embassies Berlin, Germany	010302–260805	Automatic Award

The International Diploma in Administrative Management *(Incorporated Administrator)*	080605 (40 yrs.)	The Institute of Administrative Management—*Associate Member (postnominal letters AInstAM(Dip))* *For both Education Promotion Certificates, Experience (especially British Embassy, Curriculum Vitae (Presenting Experience/Qualifications)) and Recommendation from Military Attaché Berlin (Colonel British Army)*
Defence Information Infrastructure (DII) *(ATLAS Consortium)* On behalf of: Microsoft Windows SharePoint Services	070905 (40 yrs.) 021105 031105 101105	CASH CSV8 Foundation Induction LCC LSO STS Administration (plus upgraded 191108—(43 yrs.))
Protective Document Handling Branch Information Technology Officer Unit Security Officer	241005 (40 yrs.) 271005 06–071205	Run by Intelligent Corps/Military Intelligence
Safety, Health, Environment and Fire (SHEF) and Control of Substances Hazardous to Health (COSHH)	2005–08 (40–43 yrs.)	COSHH Manual Handling Electrical Safety Checks—PAC 500—XP Fire Awareness Risk Assessments Stress and You Line Managers' Responsibilities Health and Safety in the Office Environment Desktop Computers Safety and Ergonomics
European Computer Driving Licence (ECDL)	231106 (41 yrs.)	

First Aid	190908 (43 yrs.)	German Red Cross (in English)
Microsoft Project 1 Microsoft Visio 1	26–270109 (43 yrs.) 290609 (44 yrs.)	Microsoft Qualifications
Foundation Media Course	07–110610 (45 yrs.)	Qualified Army/Military Journalist
Microsoft Windows SharePoint Services Team Site Administration	140110 (45 yrs.)	Microsoft Qualification
B1 German	0603–180713 (48 yrs.) *3 months plus*	Diploma level, Integration, required for adopting German Nationality which I did not elect to do, I remain English and (Permanent) Resident Permit level.
Certified IPC Specialist (Institute of Printed Circuits)	03/2019 (54 yrs.)	In German language

---

[1] JHQ – Joint Headquarters, Mönchengladbach, Germany

22. Military Veteran

Who is regarded as a 'Military Veteran'? Anyone who has served for at least one day,
In Her[1] Majesty's Armed Forces (Regular or Reserve) and I am an honoured veteran today.
I retired after the full 22 years' service and then, by chance, became a full-time reservist,
I was not expecting to be a full-time reservist but my ex-commanders gladly persisted.

Retired and transitioning to military veteran when the call came to re-join the service,
I gratefully went back to donning uniform for the next 54 months serving a purpose.
Promoted army journalist and in effect gave me the chance to broaden an offer,
I then volunteered to become the Royal British Legion Public Relations Officer[2].

It was here, as the RBL PRO where I was able to feel like being still, a military veteran,
My free-time, evenings and weekends as required when called for by the RBL chairman.
Steve (the chairman) *(RIP)*, also a veteran, of course, and his team of merry veterans,
More than gladly; provide financial, social and emotional support to the British Armed Forces.

Past and present and their families, and now I am a part of this remarkable organisation,
Building their website, report on events and especially the Remembrance commemorations.
The RBL is a substantial force when it comes to Remembrance Days and the Sundays,
When we visit the various military cemeteries and lay wreaths on these solemn days.

Retiring as a soldier twice sounds twice as exceptional and for that I am especially proud,
Almost 27 loyal and dedicated years' service which I pridefully shout out loud.
My family and I made many sacrifices, putting the interests of our country[3],
And the army before our own, we were rightly appreciated as we did this unreservedly.

I am fully aware of the prestigiousness of being a HM Forces Veteran in the UK,
They and their families are rightly treated favourably for the sacrifices they too have made.
I chose to retire from HM Armed Forces and reside in Germany without UK's benevolence,
My wife is German and my previous involvement with NATO[4] gave me fair precedence.

Obtaining residency was easy for me and attributable to my German qualifications, I qualify for naturalisation and it is a privilege for all of us to be a part of two nations. I chose to stay British and apply for residency every 10 years which is just a formality, The best decision; good summers, excellent medical services and a life of quality.

---

[1] In my case, Her Majesty Queen Elizabeth II.
[2] RBL PRO.
[3] My wife is a German national and my children are dual-nationality.
[4] NATO—North Atlantic Treaty Organisation.

Neal Veteran Remembrance Sunday, Reichswald Forest War Cemetery.

Neal and colleague, Veteran Remembrance Sunday Reichswald Forest War Cemetery 1/2.

Neal Veteran Remembrance Sunday Reichswald Forest War Cemetery 2/2.

ARMY

███████ SSGT N. A. ███████ AGC (SPS)

22 Years Service

On the occasion of your retirement from the Army, I wish to thank you most sincerely for the loyal service you have given.

I recognise that, in carrying out your duties as a soldier, you will have had to make many sacrifices, putting the interests of your Country and the Army before your own.

This is very much appreciated and I wish, formally, to express my gratitude for the service you have given and for the excellent contribution you have made.

I wish you all the very best for the future and every happiness in the years to come. Good luck and thank you.

Mike Jackson

Chief of General Staff

Army Form B 108X(2)
(Revised 6/00)
PPQ 50

ARMY

of Service

Surname and Number:

Testimonial (to be completed with a view to civil employment)

Mr ▇▇▇ joined the Army in 1985 and after completing basic training, served as an infantry soldier with the Queen's Lancashire Regiment. While serving in his unit, which included operational tours of duty in Northern Ireland as well as service in Germany, he undertook specialist clerical training and worked as a clerk within the unit. As part of a wider reorganisation of clerical support in the Army he transferred in 1994 to the Adjutant General's Corps, a body that provides specialist administrative, pay and human resources support to the Army.

Holding the rank of Corporal and then on promotion to Sergeant in 1996, he continued to serve in a clerical support role in infantry, engineer and logistics units within Germany, during which time he undertook two operational tours of duty to Bosnia in 1997 and Kosovo in 2000. After promotion to Staff Sergeant in 2001, he was posted as Chief Clerk to the British Military Liaison staff in Köln, affiliated to the British Embassy Berlin and then moved to the Embassy in 2002. He was instrumental in ensuring the administrative arrangements went smoothly during this difficult and complex move and had wider responsibilities for office administrative support. While in Berlin he worked as a Staff Assistant, with responsibilities in support of the formulation of policy and control for British Military Liaison officers deployed across Germany.

During his career, Mr ▇▇▇ has been a particularly fit and active soldier who has participated in a range of sporting activities, with particular achievement as a middle and long distance runner. In addition to his military administrative qualifications he has achieved a range of civilian health and safety and IT qualifications as well as achieving a Level 4 International Diploma in Administrative Management. He speaks German to a high standard.

Mr ▇▇▇'s final tour of duty with the Army has been as the Chief Clerk to the Communications and Information Systems Branch of the United Kingdom Support Command (Germany), which has pan-European infrastructure support responsibilities for the UK Defence community. This has entailed a number of reorganisations and rationalisations of office and administrative support which he has managed with great success.

Mr ▇▇▇ completes 22 years exemplary service having gained extensive experience within his Army career. He is a skilled and capable office administrator with the ability to think laterally and resolve and manage complex organisational problems. He has strong leadership skills and has the drive and determination to apply himself to a broad range of work, which makes him highly suitable for a range of potential roles and is therefore highly suitable for a wide range of employment options. He is a thoroughly reliable and trustworthy individual who is strongly recommended to any potential employer.

G6 BRANCH REGISTRY

26 OCT 2006

HQ UKSC(G)
BFPO 140

Signature of Soldier:

Signature of
Commanding Officer:

Commanding: LT COL, CH G6 BRANCH, UKSC (G)

Unit Date Stamp

TESTIMONIAL
OF
▓▓▓▓ WO2 N A ▓▓▓▓▓ AGC(SPS)

ARMY   **ARMY**

WO2 Neal ▓▓▓▓▓ joined the Army at the beginning of 1985 and after completing training, served as an Infantry Soldier with the Queen's Lancashire Regiment. While serving in his unit in Germany, he deployed on operations in Northern Ireland in 1987 and then undertook specialist skills courses to become a professional administrator and provided administrative support to a busy unit. Mr ▓▓▓▓▓ was then promoted to Lance Corporal and became a Team Leader. As part of a wider reorganisation to provide specialist office management, facilities management and personnel services (HR Human Resources), Mr ▓▓▓▓▓ transferred to the Staff and Personnel Support (SPS) Branch of the Adjutant General's Corps in Berlin in 1994. He was also assigned on short tours in Canada and Kenya.

Holding the rank of Corporal and then on promotion to Sergeant in 1996, he continued to serve as an Office Manager and operated as Chief Clerk and managed and coordinated all facilities and administrative support services and provided specialist advice and HR facilities to 100-strong Infantry, Engineer and Logistics units across Germany. During this time he undertook remote assignments to Canada and Cyprus and two peace-keeping assignments to Bosnia in 1997 and Kosovo in 2000. Mr ▓▓▓▓▓ proved to be one of the best administrators in his area of responsibility and received many Outstanding Annual Appraisals. He also ran the London Marathon for charity in 2000.

After promotion to Staff Sergeant in 2001 he was assigned to the Headquarters German Armed Forces Command in Köln as part of the British Army Liaison Organisation as their Senior Manager providing their office management and administrative expertise. Then in 2002 Mr ▓▓▓▓▓ was specially selected to transfer to a high-profile, high visibility and prestigious post to the British Embassy in Berlin representing UK diplomatic interests abroad. He directed and controlled all administrative functions and managed a team of 6 to deliver clerical support and personnel services to senior civil servants, high-ranking military officers, civil dignitaries (British, German and other Nations) and other VIP visitors. Mr ▓▓▓▓▓ delivered high-level planning and coordination activities to facilitate a smooth, problem-free and efficient service during Her Majesty the Queen's visit to Berlin in 2004. He also administered several highly successful briefings for Senior British Armed Forces Officers on behalf of the Ambassador.

During his career, Mr ▓▓▓▓▓ has been a particularly fit and active individual who participated in a range of sporting activities, with particular achievement as a middle and long distance runner. He took part in many Half Marathons and completed another full Marathon in Berlin in 2004.

His final tour as a Regular Soldier (22 years) was as Chief Clerk in the Information Communications Systems Branch of the Headquarters in Mönchengladbach providing full clerical support, office management, administrative expertise and personnel management (HR). In addition to his military administrative qualifications he has achieved a wide range of civilian Health and Safety skills including a First Aider with the German Red Cross and IT skills including ECDL and Advanced User of MS Office Suite of Productivity Tools including Visio and Project. He also achieved a Level 4 International Diploma in Administrative Management.

For over 4 years Mr ▓▓▓▓▓ was a Full Time Reservist employed as the Communications and Coordination Manager of the Media and Communications British Forces Germany Branch of the Headquarters in Mönchengladbach where he provided administrative guidance and delivered media support to the British Military across the length and breadth of Western Europe. Through his dedication, qualification and merit, he was promoted to Local Warrant Officer Class 2 which is achieved by less than 2% of personnel across all four armed services. During this tour he also passed a Foundation Media Course at the Defence Media Operations Centre at Royal Air Force Halton. He is an Incorporated Administrator and also qualifies as a Facilities Manager. He is an excellent German speaker and he is Equality and Diversity trained and Security Cleared. He is also the voluntary Public Relations Officer and Webmaster for the Rheindahlen Branch of the Royal British Legion.

Mr ▓▓▓▓▓ also has a passion for painting pictures, in particular horses and is a keen long distance cyclist participating in many cycling expeditions in Germany. He acquired significant management and leadership expertise during an Exemplary extended career spanning more than 26 years in the British Army. Mr ▓▓▓▓▓ is highly recommended to any future employer as a good team player, a calm efficient worker and an excellent person to have in a team of any size. He is a sad loss to the Army but I have no doubt he will be a prize asset to his new boss.

Signature of Soldier: *[signature]*
Signature of Commanding Officer: *[signature]* AGC
Commanding: Media & Comms BFG, HQ UKSC

Media & Comms BFG
11 JUL 2011
HQ UKSC
BFPO 140

RHINE GARRISON AND ESG NEWS
MÖNCHENGLADBACH, ELMPT, JAVELIN BARRACKS, WILDENRATH AND ESG ISODETS – WWW.BFGNET.DE/COMMUNITY/RESG

SUMMER CELEBRATION

ROYAL British Legion Rheindahlen Branch members enjoyed a sun-filled summer barbecue on Sunday, July 10, to celebrate accomplishments in this 90th Anniversary year so far.

Branch chairman Steve Reid said: "It is encouraging to see so many friends, the turn out is excellent."

The Rheindahlen Branch made a conscious effort to modernise their image, helped by their new website designed to inform a whole new group of potential supporters.

Guests of honour were the Bond van Wapenbroeders from the Netherlands who carry out ceremonial duties at war cemeteries and appropriate graves; when the Branch is on parade in the Netherlands, the Wapenbroeders are also there, and send the RBL invitations to remembrance events.

INVITATION
The Wapenbroeders were given a reciprocal invitation to join in as they have sent many invitations to the Branch for their numerous remembrance functions in the past.

Other close friends included the Motorradfreunde der Polizei (MFP) from Mönchengladbach who rode in on their bikes for the event.

Steve and the Branch secretary, Francine Garratt mingled with the crowds thanking them for making the effort for attending the sunshine party and the public relations officer for the Branch captured the smiling faces on film.

It is hoped that next year even more members and friends will be able to join in the summer festivities.

Special thanks go to Maureen Bley who worked hard to make the event such a success, Louise Cotter for her assistance and Rachel Lumley for giving up her valuable time while moving house

by Neal ▬▬▬▬
PRO RBL Rheindahlen

and faithful DJ Andy McGuire who ensured that all ages listened

● Motorradfreunde der Polizei from Mönchengladbach pictured with Branch chairman Steve Reid. Left: Steve presents a Branch pennant to Jos Korsten of the Bond van Wapenbroeders

to sounds from their own eras JB's provided the food and as ever it was excellent.

The RBL Rheindahlen Branch website is *www.RBLRheind.com*

Please visit the site and contact the Branch if we can be of any help and, of course, you wish to become a member of this prestigious organisation.

● Members, family and friends of the RBL Rheindahlen Branch enjoy the barbecue

RHINE GARRISON AND ESG NEWS
COVERING RHEINDAHLEN, MÖNCHENGLADBACH, ELMPT, JAVELIN BARRACKS, WILDENRATH AND ESG ISODETS · WWW.BFGNET.DE/COMMUNITY/RESG

A WEEK OF REMEMBRANCE

RBL's Rheindahlen Branch hold their annual Services of Remembrance

● The Service of Remembrance at the Commonwealth Military Cemetery in Reichswald was attended by civilian and military personnel and representatives from RAF JSO Det Kalkar and NATO Eihen

REMEMBRANCE week for the RBL Rheindahlen Branch area commenced with a Service of Remembrance, held on the forecourt in front of the main headquarters building at JHQ, on November 11.

General Officer Commanding United Kingdom Support Command (GOC UKSC) Maj Gen Nick Caplin gave kind permission for the Service but unfortunately was unable to attend. His wife Isobel Caplin accompanied by the British Consul General Malcolm Scott were in attendance.

Col Bill Warren, Chief of Staff UKSC, gave the Exhortation and the service was attended by people from around the garrison including officers and members of the RBL Rheindahlen Branch.

The Kohima Epitaph was given by the recently appointed President of the RBL Rheindahlen Branch, Col (Retd) Steve

by WO2 Neal ▮▮▮▮
Media & Comms BFG
Photos: Sgt Simon Butcher RAF and Dominic King

Owen. The Order of Service was given by the Reverend Canon Geoffrey Allen and Reverends Colin Craven and Nicholas Cook.

On parade were members of The Light Cavalry Band, The Band of the Royal Regiment of Scotland as well as members of The Dutch Pipes and Drums and The Crossed Swords Pipe Band.

OPPORTUNITY

After the Service invited guests attended the RBL Rheindahlen Branch buffet lunch at the Lion's Head. The opportunity of exchanging stories with many veterans was achieved.

The Remembrance week continued on Saturday, November 14 with a Service of Remembrance held at the Nederweert War Cemetery in Holland where Branch Chairman Steve Reid laid a wreath. Branch Vice Chairman Ron Pearson laid a wreath at the German Remembrance Service

in nearby Wickrath, a service attended by the Branch for the past 12 years.

These services were followed by Services of Remembrance at Reichswald War Cemetery. The Branch's public relations officer, WO2 Neal Thompson laid a wreath and the Branch Secretary Pete Richardson gave the Kohima Epitaph.

There were also services at the Rheinberg War Cemetery and the Köln Southern Cemetery. GOC UKSC Maj Gen Nick Caplin and the Branch President, Col (Retd) Steve Owen laid wreaths at the Mönchengladbach Main Cemetery with the Mayor of Mönchengladbach and other dignitaries in attendance. A service was also held at St Boniface Church, JHQ.

The Remembrance week came to a notable end on Friday, November 19 when guests attended the Post Poppy Drinks at the Lion's Head. At the Post Poppy drinks, Steve Reid explained to Maj Gen Caplin and invited guests the importance of the 'Poppy' period and the £60m the RBL spent on welfare last year.

Steve said: "Thank you for all the help, it is impossible to thank people individually in case someone is forgotten so I thank you all collectively.

"The RBL not only looks after the welfare of serving soldiers but are serving members of the Armed Forces and of course their dependants. We are aware that there will not be as much money collected this year as the Allied Rapid Reaction Corps (ARRC) has returned to the UK but nevertheless, seeing people in the NAAFI literally running their money into the collection boxes is encouraging."

Money collected this year is still to be calculated and notification of what was collected will be announced as soon as it is known.

The RBL has nearly 300,000 members worldwide with 15 Branches and a Women's Section in Germany, the most southerly of these is the Rheindahlen Branch, which was formed in 1992 and has 300 members.

The Branch meets socially every Friday at 4pm and on Sunday at 2pm in the Lion's Head, 10 Reading Way, JHQ, behind the Rheindahlen Bowl. Prospective British Legion members and their families are most welcome to pay us a visit.

● For more information contact the Branch Secretary, Pete Richardson on 02161 558 037 or email: RBLRheind@t-online.de.

● Lt Eric Smallwood, a member of A Squadron 1st Royal Tank Corps, places a poppy on the headstone of Lt Col Holliman's grave at the Remembrance Service held at the War Cemetery in Nederweert in Holland

● The mixed Bands, Pipes and Drums march passed the guests at the Remembrance Service in JHQ

● The Order of Service in JHQ was given by the Reverend Canon Geoffrey Allen and Reverends Colin Craven and Nicholas Cook

● WO2 Neal ▮▮▮▮ lays a wreath at the Reichswald War Cemetery

POPPY SUPPORT TEAMS' VITAL ROLE

IT IS EXTREMELY gratifying to know that the various charities and welfare organisations are out there in the community, including the Army Benevolent Fund and SSAFA to name but two.

But let's not forget about the other helpful organisations that are sometimes forgotten about. The Royal British Legion Poppy Support Team is one of them.

Ron Pearson is the chairman of the Poppy Support Team (Welfare) of the Rheindahlen Branch RBL and the vice chairperson is Maureen Bley. Additionally there are three 'caseworkers', namely, Karen Roskams, Liz Hein and Valerie Laucke, who have paid a huge contribution to welfare support lately. The latter two, living in Erkelenz and Geilenkirchen, carry out local visits in their areas, so saving on travelling expenses for the Legion.

HELPFUL

From September 2007 to the present day, the team has carried out almost 200 welfare visits which have either been conducted in clients' homes or visiting them in hospitals. Some meetings are also carried out on neutral ground, such as The Lions Head, in JHQ.

Liaison visits to clients' doctors and accompanying them shopping is also a regular occurrence. If the case worker did not volunteer to do this, the client would almost certainly become housebound.

Wheelchair-bound clients can also be visited on a regular basis while their family or carer is on a respite holiday.

Receiving telephone calls at all times of the day, some of which can be quite time consuming, the team are very helpful and compassionate.

Unfortunately last year, a few members of the branch passed away and attending the funerals as friends or as case workers has become a regular event. Apart from their own branch, the case workers have also attended other funerals in their case worker capacity.

In one case a sibling of a client flew in from Canada to visit her brother in a care home. The case worker acquired accommodation for her which was within her means. The lady was then taken to visit her brother in the care home on a daily basis by volunteers of the welfare team.

Where it was possible, financial assistance has been given to those in need and it can be said that in many cases, the 'client's' life has been put back on track.

Of course the case workers have to explore all avenues of possibilities before being able to apply for assistance on their behalf, but when all else fails, for example, visiting the social services offices, then their work can begin. The clients are eternally grateful to the RBL for the friendly and compassionate support which they have received. The Legion have also assisted in moving a family from Germany to the UK recently, which all happened within one month.

TRAVELLED

During the last financial year, the Poppy Support Team, Royal British Legion Rheindahlen Branch, has travelled thousands of kilometres on welfare cases.

Well done to Ron and his dedicated Poppy Support Team: Karen Roskams, Val Laucke, Ron Pearson (Chairman), Maureen Bley (Vice-Chairperson) and Liz Hine, who are pictured at the RBL centre in Rheindahlen Camp.

● Don't forget that the Royal British Legion is out there to serve ex-Servicemen and women in need, so if you want to get in touch, visit the Royal British Legion website: *www.britishlegion.org.uk*

● The Poppy Support Team RBL Rheindahlen Branch: From left, Karen Roskams, Val Laucke, Chairman Ron Pearson, Vice-Chairperson Maureen Bley and Liz Hine

Story by
WO2 Neal ▆▆▆▆
PRO RBL
Rheindahlen Branch

23. Civvy Street

I commenced this short tale on 5 January 2024, 39 years ago to the day,
Since walking through those barrack gates and receiving my army pay.

The words 'Civvy Street' mean nothing to most of you, it's a British army term,
We use the term to refer to life and work which is not connected to us in the firm.

I was in the army for 27 years so I use this jargon regularly, it is what I know,
'Fizz' is fitness, 'leave' is holiday and 'scoff' and 'egg banjo' are food so there you go.
Getting 'fizzed' too much would be a 'beasting' and 'KFS' is knife fork and spoon,
If you have something spare; equipment, we call that 'buckshee' in the platoon.
When tired from our 'stag' (guard duty), "stag on mate," we get our heads down,
Combats, boots still on and dirty and climb into our 'doss bags' on the ground.
'End Ex[1]' is probably our favourite, and when you are selfish[2], we call that 'jack,'
'Green' is 'keen' and when you have a story to tell we say, "pull up a sandbag."

There was just a few to get you on your way and the main aim of this short tale,
My first real job on 'Civvy Street' was aged 48[3] and that thankful letter in the mail.

After leaving school, I did a couple of youth training schemes until I found my way,
I left the army in autumn 2011 and elected to reside in Germany until present day.
I took a year out, enjoying long walks with my dog 'Bonnie' and then back to school,
A few months learning proper German full-time (Grade B1) which you need as a rule.
You require this qualification for your 'naturalisation' or at least your 'resident permit,'
Another fine entry on my colourful CV[4] so off to the job centre to find jobs that fit.

I was referred to a leasing agent, 'Kangaroo' to be exact, as leasing is the way to go,
In my time, it was quite normal to go through these channels, as it is, who you know.
My Interview went well and they referred me to a local company in Erkelenz, Mektec[5],
I did the obvious revision from the net as you do, it was very impressive and high-tech.
Mektec GmbH make Flexible Printed Circuits (FPC) and after interview, Q&A and a tour,
Like a first job, I was so grateful when I received the welcome letter through my door.

I started with day shift and naturally I was nervous and it was daunting to say the least,
Issued with footwear, blue trousers and grey jacket and then introduced to the beast.
The beast was a hell of a machine, giant heated rollers where the copper goes through,
The department was called 'Kalander' and it was the first stage of the production too.
The German language was hard, especially combining it with the learning but I got it,
It took a few months to learn and then pass the training but all in all, I was a good fit.
Well and truly on the roster now and starting to do proper shifts; earlies, lates and nights,
This is 'civvy street' for you, working in a factory and working shifts but I hated nights.
The worst thing about nights was the fact that your performance and production,
Must be the same as the other shifts which I found absurd as it was harder to function.
Nevertheless, I got on with it without 'bumping' (moaning) and eventually proved an asset,
The company offered me my first-year contract and then my second so my life was set.
The rule was that at your third-year point you would receive a permanent contract or let go,
This is where life got a little complicated as my department was moving away, "oh no."

Kalander was being transferred to our sister company in the (CZ) Czech Republic,
It was part of a reorganisation and in hindsight, thank God I could speak English.
The company wanted me to train the Czech workers before the machine moved,
I trained them the best I could and it was sad when the machine was removed.
The company then offered me a permanent contract if I would go to CZ to teach,
I obviously accepted to go for a few weeks as my contract was within my reach.
Off I went in the company BMW 800 km southeast to České Budějovice (Budweis),
The drive was long and hard and after a couple of breaks, 12 hours later, I arrived.
I ended up doing this trip a couple of times over a couple of months, living in a hotel,
I actually enjoyed my time there, teaching and report-writing and I did quite well.
The group from Germany and the guys from Budweis enjoyed each other socially,
I recommend Budweis, the €uro went a long way and great food and beer totally.
Mektec CZ offered for me to stay there full-time and also paid with a German salary,
I thought about it and after a discussion with my wife, the answer was no in reality.

The new reality was returning to Mektec Erkelenz and learning a new position,
In short, I tried various FPC cleaning stations and then the soldering section.
At this stage, I developed a problem with my hip and had to undergo an operation,
My previous time in the army, my running hobby and heavy-lifting was the realisation.
The hip-replacement put me out for a few months but I returned keen and raring to go,
My new job in the AOI[6] branch was interesting, inspecting production as part of the flow.
After approximately 12 months or so, unfortunately, my hip-replacement came loose,
On investigation, it was realised there were germs inside my hip which was bad news.

The hip-replacement was replaced again, a 6-hour operation followed by intensive care,
After months of rehabilitation and physiotherapy I was trying to get back to work to be fair.
With my qualifications, I offered to work in quality assurance but there was no job for me,
The hard work in CZ was now going to waste and the job they offered, we could not agree.
With a 30% disability grade and no more heavy-lifting meant I could no longer work there,
By mutual agreement, I had no choice but to resign which was really hard to bear.

On an end note, my assumption on 'civvy street' is that non-smokers do all the work,
Camaraderie does not exist and loyalty is out of the window, I say, with a smirk.
Civvies fend for themselves, and trust for me, is now a thing of the past,
Early retirement it is then, as good things never last.

---

[1] End Ex—is called when we are at the end of a military exercise or other manoeuvre and/or military operation.

[2] I am being very polite with the word 'selfish.'

[3] My standing joke is that I did not get a 'proper' job (other than the army) until the grand old age of 48.

[4] CV is 'Lebenslauf' in German and it really is quite different, in effect, it is just a chronological list of what you have done really rather than a full description/summary.

[5] Mektec Manufacturing Corporation Europe DE GmbH.

[6] AOI—Automatic Optical Inspection.

Mektec Erkelenz 1/2.

Mektec Erkelenz 2/2.

24. Military Medals

It has to be a real honour to be awarded a military medal and I am very proud,
Those people who have been awarded them certainly stand out in a crowd.
It is a shame that I only have 4 whereas many of my former comrades-in-arms,
Rightly had many more as they had been crucially deployed in more harms.
Suspended in descending[1] order as I would wear them on the left side of my chest,
In the past wearing best dress[2] or mess dress and today as a veteran smartly dressed.

Ribbons of the same design (without the medals) are just as significant to wear,
Ribbons also serve to highlight the status and significance of the award you bear.
In my case, my four medals are block-mounted together as one complete form,
There were 2 sewn loops just above the stitched-on ribbons on my dress uniform.
With the long pin behind the medals, they were looped through the loops there,
The medals suspended proudly on my chest and were shown off to all who stare.

Let us not forget the clasp on the medal sometimes known as Campaign Bars,
The military campaign involves a series of operations and a phrase of wars.
A large-scale long-duration significant military strategy plan incorporating,
A series of interrelated military operations or battles or even peacekeeping.
Certain medals have your service number, rank, name, initials and regiment,
Diamond engraved on the edge of the medal and a much-treasured sentiment.

You now know the description of a medal and now I will share mine with you,
The first medal I was awarded was the 1962 General Service Medal, silver too.
The obverse shows the crowned effigy of Queen Elizabeth II and the reverse,
Bears the words 'FOR CAMPAIGN SERVICE' under a crown, all encompass.
By a wreath of oak leaves and my service details on the edge of it are seen,
With 'NORTHERN IRELAND' clasp and the ribbon is purple edged with green.

That was 1987 and the next 2 medals of the late 1990s, I will couple together,
The NATO[3] Medal with 'FORMER YUGOSLAVIA' Clasp for peacekeeping in Bosnia.
And, the NATO Medal with 'KOSOVO' clasp for peacekeeping in the Balkans,
Made of bronze and bearing the NATO star and set in a wreath of olive leaves.

The reverse has the NATO title and 'IN SERVICE OF PEACE AND FREEDOM,'
With blue and white ribbons, each of similar designs distinguishing them.

My final medal was the 2002 Golden Jubilee Medal, "Thank You, Your Majesty,"
"Marking a major milestone of 50 years of service Ma'am, your Golden Jubilee."
Cupro-nickel with a gilt finish and again, the obverse with Her Majesty's effigy,
My service details are on its edge with a red, white and blue ribbon, traditionally.
Regrettably, there are medals that evaded me, I say, "the ones that got away,"
An imperfect soldier with one medal in particular which plays on my mind to this day.

The Long Service and Good Conduct Medal for 15 years of Reckonable Service,
Unblemished service obviously and as a private soldier I did a great disservice.
At the beginning of my service, I was admittedly naive and did not take life seriously,
Whereas, after 15 years and promoted through the ranks, my service was exemplary.
One can apply for it and my application was supported by my commanding officer,
You can also apply on retirement but unfortunately, it evaded me, I have my four.

I was on standby to deploy to Gulf War 1 and on holiday when my name was called,
I was abroad at the time and another soldier went in my place and I was appalled.
I was there for our son's beginning when Gulf War 1 and the medal escaped me,
I was in protected positions working in the embassy for Gulf War 2 thankfully.
And in JHQ[4] when the final medal eluded me; the OS[5] Medal for Afghanistan,
As parents, it was hard when our son deployed there twice, *he is a brave man.*

---

[1] Descending order, the order you received the medals.
[2] No. 1 Dress, or "dress blues" is a ceremonial uniform. No. 2 Dress or "khaki" is the main parade uniform. Mess Dress is the formal military evening dress (you would wear miniature military medals for this dress).
[3] NATO—North Atlantic Treaty Organisation.
[4] JHQ—Joint Headquarters, Mönchengladbach, Germany.
[5] OS—Operational Service.

My four military medals.

Col 'Mike' and me (Neal) Berlin, Germany. No1 Best Dress 'Blues' with medals.

HRH State Visit to Germany Nov 2004, at British Embassy Berlin. Me (Neal) and family. No2 Service Dress. Just the ribbon and not the medals.

Lt Col 'Luke' and me (Neal) at the Gala Concert, Berlin HRH State Visit to Germany Nov 2004. Mess Dress with miniature medals.

Neal and Veteran colleague—Remembrance Sunday Reichswald Forest War Cemetery. Civilian Dress with medals.

25. Remembrance (Another Synonym)

Both of my parents passed away in 2018 which left an enormous hole in my world,
Sadly, they were long divorced but lived in the same town, which we all preferred.
My mum departed us on Valentine's Day and my dad passed away nearly 3 months later,
What is also sad is this short gap is irrelevant really as they never saw each other.

Living in Germany meant that I was unable to say my last goodbye to them both,
This still plays on my mind but my conscience is clear as I could not get home.
Their demises did bring the remainder of my family together though, which is worthy,
We siblings are not all close and some were not close to our parents, somewhat murky.

The journeys from Germany to the UK for their funerals were so unforgettable,
Their respective funerals were so sad but the wakes were so respectable.
All of us sat there in a bunch, swapping memories of Mum then Dad and laughing,
Traditionally clinking glasses of something and eating cake as we were all reminiscing.

When I was in the army, I probably saw them annually but since I retired, not so,
Their last couple of years were not memorable and sadly their morale was low.
Moving from their own homes to nursing homes must have been devastating,
But they could not live alone anymore as their dependencies were accelerating.

My dad was born in Liverpool in 1932 and at 8, he donned his Mickey Mouse gas mask,
One of Dad's memories, and when he was a man, he enlisted for his national service ask.
I, like my dad, am averagely small in height but to me, Dad was still a tower of a man,
He was tough with us growing up when Mum left home and he was the 'chief' of the clan.
When I was a kid, he called me 'Twiggy' because I was skinny and his daughter 'Fluff Ball,'
My favourite bro was his 'Mini-Me' in my view, he too, like me, does not stand tall.
When I left home, I still went back home often, especially when I was a soldier,
We wrote to each other and had many meaningful chats, particularly as I grew older.
He was well read and his knowledge on current affairs and horse-racing was prodigious,
His love of music, especially 'Ol' Blue Eyes' and his music collection was boundless.
His eyes lit up when I arrived in from Germany with an exported litre of Glayva,
You could not buy a litre of his favourite liqueur in the UK and he loved its flavour.

My last memory of Dad was shortly before he was admitted to a nursing home,
Marion and I visited him and as though we were not there, he sat down on his own.
Dad was watching TV instead of stood at the kitchenette reading his papers,
And, listening to his music as he reads the news from the press news-shapers.
His flat used to be spick and span and he could now not hold a conversation,
He always looked forward to us visiting but this time was a new realisation.
We said farewell and that I would see him in the next few days and left him there,
We did not go back and see him as we thought it futile but he was indeed aware.
I cannot go back and change this but I know we loved each other undeniably,
I have many hilarious memories of our drinking and dancing as his life was a party.

My wonderful mum was born in Ackworth, West Yorkshire on leap year 1936,
She would jokingly boast about her actual age but we all knew which age sticks.
My children growing up would refer to Grandma as posh and that she was a real lady,
She left home when I was 9 but she had her reasons and I forgave her, my milady.
She stayed local at first until she moved to the south and then to NAAFI[1] in Germany,
I missed her in those days but at least she was happy there and found harmony.
We too had a beautiful relationship, both before and after I joined the army,
My best memories were when we all met up with my wife and children, it was lovely.
I always said she was the best mum ever until *we* had children of course,
My mum's cooking is always referred to and she will always be in my thoughts.
My wife Marion totally respected her and called her 'Mum,' very naturally,
I found that so respectful and my children were besotted by her adorably.
My children could not wait for her to visit, especially my daughters and her makeup,
We made many trips together to wonderful places and my lad and her man were made-up.
Mum had an absolute great mind with her crosswords, embroidery, knitting and Scrabble,
I never ever beat her at Scrabble, I think I needed more training and just babbled.
I know that she really was a *model* mother and also a good singer and dancer,
At least I saw her singing many times and I even have her songs here and I hear her.
I found it special to call her for a chat and send her flowers for the 3 times a year,
When I told her some of my favourite lyrics (for a tattoo) 'rubbish' she cheered.
A peculiar memory perhaps, and when I visited her at the nursing home, it was bad,
Mum did not recognise her favourite son or his wife which broke our hearts, so sad.

Disease	**A**bnormal	**C**anker
Exercising	**L**oneliness	**A**cute
Memory	**Z**estless	**N**asty
Engagement	**H**untington's	**C**ells
Needy	**E**arly-onset/stage	**E**vil
Thinking	**I**ncontinence	**R**andom
Impair	**M**ental Illness	
Abilities	**E**ldercare	
	Remembrance	
	Socially	

For the challenged mind, I have created a 'Word Search' overleaf.

---

[1] NAAFI—Navy, Army and Air Force Institutes.

Word Search

```
C O G N I T I V E Z Z I P Q A X K R Z J D F V C
I E C O P S Q U O M N C M U P S Q E G B E R L O
P R E L I F E S T Y L E A P R S Q L A E P O K M
T I E L A G E I N G J B N O A P M I C H P N A P
I H J L F A M I L Y P S A Z R I O A T A R T L A
N N I K A M P O E T R Y D A S T R N I V E O Z S
D J J N T M D E M E N T I A P S T V I S T H S
E A Y I K O I E X E R C I S I N G S I O S E E I
P L B F Q I A O S Q D E C L I N E A T U I M I O
E E J N K L N M N P L D I S E A S E I R O P M N
N I L M O F D G G S U O I V S T I O E W N O E A
D S U O P R S T V D H A N S A J H J S K B R R T
E U H R S Q M A S A J I Z E Q S G O H I O A S E
N R M N Q T C A V X B C P C L W C T B X N L N M
T E Q J B A I O L K B I S S F I H U S B H B N F
C O M B A T T I N G Q Q L S S G N Q L H I J K E
R E M E M B R A N C E J K I Q P Z E E A O E S S
B N M E M O R Y Z L O S S J T G O H S Q R D S L
C O M M U N I C A T E Q H N V I S R Q S H J M I
A A G G R E S S I O N S S T Y E E B T W A L D N
H U N T I N G T O N S P P F J R E S I S S O I G
P U Z Z L E S R W R I T I N G T Y J K A Q V E S
E N G A G E M E N T R E M E M B E R A R W E T D
J K H Q L E W Y D B O D Y F G J E R O T U S W T
```

Words to Find

LEWY	BODY	VASCULAR
BEHAVIOUR	FEELINGS	COMBATTING
PUZZLES	REMEMBER	IMPAIR
THINKING	DEMENTIA	COMPASSIONATE
ABILITIES	REMEMBRANCE	SPORTS
HOBBIES	LIFESTYLE	FRONTOTEMPORAL
RELIANT	COGNITIVE	LOVE
WRITING	LEISURE	ALZHEIMERS
POETRY	LONELINESS	INDEPENDENT
ABNORMAL	MEMORY	LOSS
FAMILY	COMMUNICATE	ART
ACTIVITIES	RELATIONSHIPS	LOST
DECLINE	AGGRESSION	HUNTINGTONS
DEPRESSION	AGEING	EXERCISING
DISEASE	DIET	ENGAGEMENT

Word Search (Solution)

C	O	G	N	I	T	I	V	E			I					R			D	F		C
											M					E		B	E	R		O
	R	L	I	F	E	S	T	Y	L	E		P				L	A	E	P	O		M
T		E		A	G	E	I	N	G				A			I	C	H	P	N	A	P
I	H		L	F	A	M	I	L	Y					I		A	T	R	R	T	L	A
N		I		A		P	O	E	T	R	Y				R	N	I	V	E	O	Z	S
D			N		T	M	D	E	M	E	N	T	I	A		T	V	I	S	T	H	S
E	A			K		I	E	X	E	R	C	I	S	I	N	G	I	O	S	E	E	I
P	L	B			I		O		D	E	C	L	I	N	E		T	U	I	M	I	O
E	E		N		N	M		L	D	I	S	E	A	S	E		I	R	O	P	M	N
N	I	L		O		G		S		O		V				E		N	O	E	A
D	S		O		R		T		H		N		A		H	J	S		R	R	T
E	U		R	S		M		A		I	Z	E		S	G				A	S	E
N	R		T		A		B		P		L		C		B			L		
T	E		L			I		S		I		H		U		B				F
C	O	M	B	A	T	T	I	N	G		L		S		N		L	I		E
R	E	M	E	M	B	R	A	N	C	E		I		P		E	A	E		E
	M	E	M	O	R	Y		L	O	S	S		T		O		S	R	S	L
C	O	M	M	U	N	I	C	A	T	E				I		R		S		I
	A	G	G	R	E	S	S	I	O	N				E		T		L	D	N
H	U	N	T	I	N	G	T	O	N	S				S		S		O	I	G
P	U	Z	Z	L	E	S		W	R	I	T	I	N	G		A		V	E	S
E	N	G	A	G	E	M	E	N	T	R	E	M	E	M	B	E	R		E	T
				L	E	W	Y		B	O	D	Y						T		

26. Pets IV

In commemoration, and celebrating our pets and their wonderful and loyal lives.
The poems below (in seniority order) intentionally intertwine with each other.

I—Bes (Mixed Border Collie) (15)

Bes was about two when I was introduced to her when my boss asked if I wanted her,
  She belonged to a colleague who could no longer keep her, and oh how sad we were.
I took Bes home and introduced her to Marion and Vanessa and asked if she could stay,
It was a very easy decision; she was so good with us so we just couldn't send her away.
My dad was temporarily living with us and used to love taking Bes on his long walks,
  The Yorkshire moors were next to us and Dad and the angry farmers had many talks.

Then came baby Matthew, another human for her to deal with and Dad moved out,
  Dad moved into his own place so we took Bes with us to see him out and about.
Dad went back to Burnley and we left for Germany, probably Bes's first time abroad,
Berlin winters are harsh and unfortunately, she couldn't play out proper until it thawed.
She had to endure quarantine, it is so hard for pets and so unnecessary, a past UK con,
A needless few months away from family but luckily, settling back in didn't take too long.

My dad came to visit and the first thing he wanted to do was take Bes out somewhere,
  Dad, Matthew, Bes and I went for a jolly to the park and lake and enjoying the fresh air.
Matthew was on the kid's death-slide, Grandad and I taking care that he didn't fall,
Then we would throw sticks for Bes as she is swimming in the lake, oh what a ball.
  She loved to come running with me no matter how far my training runs took us,
  When we got back home and everyone greeted us, she really loved all the fuss.

She was my first running mate and I had plenty of water bottles on my belt to share,
I couldn't take her on the real races and she was so upset when I just left her there.
The big change for her was when her brother moved in, welcome to Simba the cat,
Then Hannah was born, Bes was probably wondering what is going on and all that.
Eventually back in Berlin and retired from running with me and a puppy is her new test,
Bonnie moved in and later Bes died from illness and old age and was sadly laid to rest.

II—Simba (Half Persian) (16)

After watching the animated film *Lion King*, it put us in the mood to get a kitten,
We drove to Laarbruch air base[1] to collect him and we were really quite smitten.
He was a brownish-gold and white half Persian, the little thing was just adorable,
Marion's cat settled in very quickly and the prince was completely unignorable.
Nala moved in next door but you could say that Simba never batted an eyelid,
Nala was not his mate and in our version of Pride Rock, there won't be a kid.

Simba was not really afraid of her big sister and dominated Bes eventually,
Bes was often told what to do or what not to do in animal language, *probably*.
Pretty much Marion's cat so I left her to it, he was now her responsibility,
He was not afraid of me and protected his mum when I was there, with hostility.
The outdoor cat presented himself to his traffic and Marion had to intervene,
Stopping the traffic to retrieve him from the opposite side, mediating in-between.

Cool, calm and collected; his smooth coat was unruffled when he hurdled fences,
Rattling his scoff box out back to bring him home and watching him at his races.
When I was allowed in his presence, he would watch Matthew and I build his truck,
Simba supervised us constructing with K'nex, waiting to ride it and then get stuck.
Standing at the fish tank speculating what is on his menu and senses the tasting,
He will have to wait for a long time as the fish dishes are pretty much still swimming.

It was sadly time for his castration and our neighbours submitted a signed petition,
There were plenty of signatures to save his poor nuts, a proved failing opposition.
Recovering and not allowed to play out, missing his admiring fans; the butterflies,
Lolling around on the kid's beds and choosing Hannah's cradle and happily cries.
Promoted to stopping tractors outside the house and sharing a roof with his rival,
Simba was very ill in his good old age and there was sadly no chance for his survival.

III—Bonnie (Pharaoh Hound Whippet Mix) (16)

We gladly adopted a puppy that originally came from a shelter home in Barcelona,
She wasn't our first choice and wasn't particularly comely and sat there like a loner.
She was typically daft and Bes let her know it despite her old age and fragility,
Bonnie settled in very quickly and now the training begins to identify her ability.
She definitely grew on you and eventually you had to succumb to her uniqueness,
You could say that she was actually cute in her own little way, a sort of prettiness.

When big sister Bes passed on, there was sadness in Bonnie's eyes, cradle to grave,
The circle of life is sad, her first teacher had left her and her path was now paved.
I took her running with me, she quickly developed into my second running mate,
When off the lead she was much faster than Bes and she was proving to be as great.
When we went on holiday, Bonnie also went on vacation to a pet place with a pool,
Bes had one on her as Bonnie couldn't swim, but had fun playing around like a fool.

She never minded sharing her bed with the boss; her big-little brother Simba the cat,
Simba was seniority now and let Bonnie know occasionally that he was king and all that.
Living in the Headquarters[2] was when she decided to run away with the dog next door,
Bonnie's excuse when caught was she was just chasing rabbits and her defence was poor.
When I retired from serious running and then the army, Bonnie was my unpaid walker,
Watching fields change their theme was when we bumped into the stranded kitten talker.

A new little sister Chummy at home and Bonnie and Simba were watching her closely,
Simba sadly passed from old age and Chummy and Bonnie had lost their one and only.
Just Bonnie and Chummy now, sharing a bed or space and we retired from long walks,
Best friend Hannah allowed her on her bed and hearing them conspiring in their talks.
Hard of hearing but Bonnie quickly learned sign then sadly no longer allowed off the leash,
It was so sad when she died from illness and old age and we miss her dearly, rest in peace.

IV—Chummy (Feral Born?) (13)

When I was walking the dog one day near our home, we heard a very shallow meow,
I looked around and I saw the smallest and cutest thing ever, was it really a kitten, wow!
It toddled over to me and sat near my foot meowing and scared and presumably feral,
Seemingly only a few weeks old and where it walked out from the bushes was sheer peril.
Seeing its dead white sibling was so sad so I just had to take this one home to the flock,
Marion and Hannah stared and wondered what I had in my arms, wrapped in my sock.

Plan A was to take it to the vet for a check-up and off to the animal home, and Plan B?
The girls brought it back home and told me that it was staying and that it was a 'she.'
I christened her Chummy after an old family cat of the same name when I was a child,
The girls liked her new name and Marion was traditionally bottle-feeding her as we smiled.
Chummy was a chatterbox and always up for a discussion and over time, she adopted me,
Her last few months were hard for her but she really tried to be herself in her brave plea.

Giving her as much care as possible was a real privilege, honoured palliative care, Although inevitable, there was always room for a prayer but finally needing to prepare. Chummy was only 13 when she died from cancer and she left a huge hole in my heart, I think of her past and how she enjoyed life and I thank her for letting me take part. When she passed on, and also for the first time, I visited the place where ***she found me***, I just stood there for a while and said a few words, "she is not ill anymore and free."

She knew when we were coming home and although quiet, could hear us at the door, Chummy walked out on her own accord and scratched her nails on the mat on the floor. She was so loyal and I will never forget her and inseparable best friends, we truly were, Chummy was cremated and when out and about, I think of her in the air and talk to her. She would scream to get out onto the balcony despite understanding the varied weather, The balcony was her place so we have a plaque out there now to remember her forever.

Epilogue:—No more pets now and no more sadness. You have to imagine the changes they have to go through if they have siblings and then the siblings pass away. Then the children grow up and leave home. ***The Circle of Life of Cradle to Grave.*** We currently have Chewy (Hannah's cat) over sometimes for sleepovers and we used to dog-sit next door's dog until she sadly died. Now, that's lots of paws for thought!

---

[1] Laarbruch—Royal Air Force (RAF) air base, now it is Weeze Airport, near Düsseldorf, Germany.
[2] Headquarters—Joint Headquarters, Mönchengladbach, Germany.

Bes 1/2.

Bes 2/2.

Simba 1/2.

Simba 2/2.

Bonnie.

Hannah and Bonnie.

Simba and Chummy.

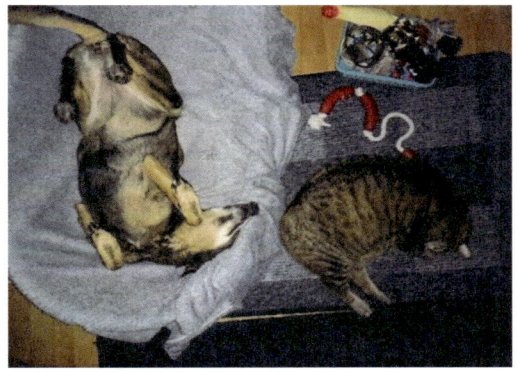

Bonnie and Chummy.

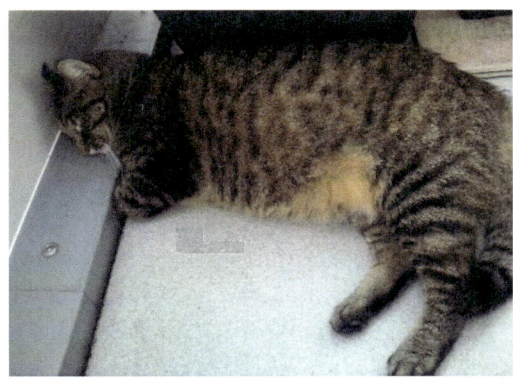

Chummy.

27. Shooting Stars

We take our glittering dark sky for granted because it is always there,
The orbiting moon shines through and gives us a light and warm glare.
A shooting star is most wondrous but it is sadly over in seconds,
And we only see them if we look into the vastness of the heavens.
The rapidly moving meteor burns up on entering our atmosphere,
And it means many things to us if we use our imagination here.
The rock arrives from space and glows as it is streaking across our view,
This beautiful time as space is rejoicing, I am sure you have seen one too.
There are roughly 6 per hour that can be seen anywhere on Earth,
They symbolise many things, endings and beginnings, conceivably birth.
A blank canvas presenting darkness above as we long for the beauty,
Twinkling stars and a shooting star inspires feelings of awe and humility.
Just imagine two lovers lying in an open space peering up into the night sky,
And, when they do see a shooting star as it entwines their true love up high.
Perhaps a shooting star brings luck and grants wishes to receive,
A shooting star can mean many things as long as you just believe.
When (and not if) you see one it can give you hope or a message,
It can mean many things, anything you want or simply safe passage.
Embracing your journey will guide you towards your life's goals,
This magical mystical phenomena whispers through our souls.
The descriptions above are but a few of what a shooting star brings,
Look after each other and love one another as our Mother Earth sings.

When I was a teenager walking back down from Peter's grandma up Tum Hill,
I think this was my earliest memory of seeing a shooting star and what a thrill.
We both discussed what we had seen and what it means and just guessed,
Talking of luck, wishes, dreams of fortune and perhaps aspiring to be the best.

This verse in-between is time, many years of time where I must have seen one,
I must have seen shooting stars, many of them, I simply must have done.
From my travels, where I was fortunate to see many a starry sky somewhere,
Canada, Kenya, Bosnia, Cyprus and Egypt as I was possibly unaware.

This is where we take life for granted and perhaps a shooting star is a norm,
Where these incredible happenings flare through the dark sky like a storm.
The truth is, if you look into the dark sky long enough, you should see one,
They have flashed through our space for a lifetime, since time begun.

My next memory was my niece's 21st birthday when I was in Kosovo,
I recall sending her a SMS and then what do you know.
We saw a shooting star as we found ourselves staring into 'space 1999,'
Like kids, us soldiers were so happy of what we saw in this place and time.
We were having a squadron campfire on a restful summer's night,
Probably having our earned '2-beers rule' so the timing was just right.

I have actually seen one or two from my balcony here over the years,
Warm late nights and normally sat alone and giving space a 'cheers.'
These days, as I talk to myself, the space and the shooting star, I say,
"My wife appears to have not seen one and I hope she does one day."

28. Role Reversal

I have an announcement to make, "I have been *smugly* promoted again,"
You all wait in anticipation to hear what I am going to broadcast then.
I have been promoted to 'househusband'; Mr Mop or Janitor Joe,
Whatever name you wish to say, I am not embarrassed, you know.

After 27 years being a soldier and a time on 'civvy street[1],' what now?
I can be the 'househusband,' it can't be that hard, teach me how.
A sort of forced early retirement at 58, and now time for a change,
To be honest, I have been doing this for a while now, I like to rearrange.

OCD[2] (NO!), I find putting things into their order is sort of therapeutic,
I feel that OCD is a sort of illness of which it is not, I am simply symmetric.
I just like things to be straight because everything has a place,
Putting things here and there is simple, as everything has a space.

So, the chores should be relatively easy although I will do things my way,
I dust at the end of the housework which is wrong apparently, who is to say?
Everyone has their own systems, I just use military discipline and analysis,
It is what I know, it is my past, **sometimes** I am just joking and taking the p**s.

I have the routine down to a tee, exactly and to perfection and no one there,
Alone with Alexa to keep me company, I tell her to "play music everywhere."
The daily routine is simple, tidy, empty the dishwasher and hoover my grounds,
The weekly routine includes dusting, toilets and requires my favourite sounds.

If I am honest, it is much easier nowadays with the tools they offer for a price,
I can't do the dusting without my Swiffer[3], excellent against dust, very nice.
Use a steam mop, perhaps an expensive one-off item at first, just add water,
It doesn't leave any streaks and you save on other soaps etc; I hear laughter.

Who would have thought that 'Block Jobs[4]' in the army would come in handy?
Now responsible for everything 'housework' at home and doing the laundry.
It is only fair to **role reverse** when wifey goes to work, this stuff is not for her,
"*Her* weekends and holidays now," in the past with me, it was how things were.

Washing was a challenge, a bit technical plus separating darks and lights,
Some people don't do that seemingly, add bubble paper and whites stay white.
It took a while to memorise the different settings but now I am a bit of a whizz,
Some people just chuck in their washing and hope for the best, it is what it is.

Ironing is a bit flat (pardon the unintended pun) but is a necessary bore,
I did enough ironing in the army so I know what an iron is and what it is for.
Some people don't bother with ironing stuff but I think it is a requirement,
Now folding the nicely ironed stuff is an art, something I proudly present.

Now, sewing is a skill I am proud of, so obviously I am nominated at home,
Hannah doesn't go to Mum for that, she comes to the notorious needle gnome.
Buttons and holes have nothing on me, bring it on I say, I like the contest,
Even Hannah's shoe straps fixed and also her dress, she was so impressed.

Cooking escaped me, I never needed to master that, apart from the obvious,
Pot noodles, cup-a-soup, beans on toast and toasties are my main course.
But I am a SME[5] (Subject Matter Expert) at party plates, a master creation,
Sandwich squares, bits of salad and crisps and whatever else is my invention.

Whilst the kids haven't mastered Mum's cooking yet, they can all do party plates,
They do well with their tasty delights and Vanessa makes lovely biscuits and cakes.
The SME continues with salads of sorts and proficient with the cold stuff at least,
I make a mixed salad with a certain acquired taste and I truly am the salad beast.

I suppose it would be rude of me if I didn't share the 'tricks of the trade,'
For me, it is easy, keeping the home spick and span is like being on parade.
Do wash separately, do iron your tea-towels, do listen to your partner or wife,
Buff[6] your sinks, taps and shower after use; your water, your mess, such is life.

To conclude this short story then, you could say there were lessons learned,
And becoming the 'househusband' of the year is something you have earned.
You are not just a man, you are a very useful man and a man of all needs,
Making plants too, there is more to you than simply planting your seeds.

Endnote from the poet: I recommend placing a couple of sheets of kitchen roll in the bottom of your pedal bin bag to soak up stuff in case your bag is punctured. God help us all when I get a systems malfunction (laughing-out-loud)!

---

[1] People in the armed forces use civvy street to refer to life and work which is not connected with armed forces.

[2] OCD—obsessive-compulsive disorder is a common, chronic, and long-lasting disorder in which a person has uncontrollable, reoccurring thoughts ("obsessions") and/or behaviours ("compulsions") that he or she feels the urge to repeat over and over.

[3] Swiffer—https://www.swiffer.com to view all products.

[4] Block Jobs—in the army is a definition for cleaning your block accommodation from top to bottom, everything. Windows, floors, toilets, sinks and showers. Not forgetting your own private spaces. Nowadays, there is a cleaner who does it for you and there is no more 'block beds and hospital corners,' now you have your own quilts. Bless & Bliss!

[5] SME—Subject Matter Expert is a military term (I believe).

[6] Buff—To clean or polish (metal) or give a grainless finish of high lustre to (plated surfaces) with or as if with a buff stick or buff wheel, in my case, simply your towel.

29. Regrets

Unfortunately, everyone has regrets, it's simply a part of the human condition,
Feeling sad or sorry about something that you did or did not do is just an emotion.
We too have contentment, a satisfaction or happiness which evens it all out,
And, we do not have to avoid regret at all costs as it is what life is all about.

I very much regret not doing better with education and sport at school,
My priorities were flirting and smoking I suppose and thought I was being cool.
I enlisted into the army where I completed my education and ran marathons,
As parents, we believe we guided our children the right way in comparisons.

I regret not being there more for my wife, especially in our children's early years,
Deployed somewhere and Marion playing both parents and wiping their tears.
Behind every married soldier, there is a wife with real strength beside him[1],
The best wife and mother ever and through thick and thin, we'll always win.

The army is a commitment and my family and I made many sacrifices, all of us,
When I deployed on operations to Bosnia, I missed Hannah's first Christmas.
I regret missing her dance to 'Cotton Eye Joe' and Matthew taking part in 'Grease,'
At least I saw him singing 'Eminem' and Vanessa easily out-singing our niece.
We all watched Matthew graduating from Army College, a family at their proudest,
We regret Vanessa going to the UK and glad she returned to us and found happiness.
We saw Hannah graduating from college and thankful Vanessa gave us grandchildren,
We are so grateful that they are all doing great with their respective partners, well done.
We have probably hundreds of hours of home movies which are readily there,
When we have those moments watching them, we can't help but laugh and stare.

Comparing to my comrades-in-arms, I really was home with family most of the time,
Alike, when I was away, it gave me other opportunities and I had some good times.
I do not regret staying at the embassy and theoretically turning down promotion,
My family and my commanders there were equally content that I made that decision.

Like most children, I regret not seeing my parents more, especially their final years,

Abroad and unable to say goodbye when they passed and sharing my siblings' tears.
I was a good son and saw them as often as possible and it was mostly reciprocal,
At least they knew I loved them and writing to Dad and telephoning Mum was typical.
I regret that my siblings and I do not see each other more, especially one or two,
I miss my favourite bro and only sister and especially when they needed me too.

Regretfully retiring from running, withdrawing from a marathon for medical reasons,
Running was my passion and, in those days, I would be out training in all seasons.
Restricted nowadays but nevertheless still a fitness freak looking for a challenge,
And able to cycle 200km from Trier to Koblenz over 2 days put my life into balance.

I regret having tattoos and if I could go back in time, I would not have any,
I like body art and there are good designs, but not covered and not too many.
Marion and the kids have them which is okay by me as they are fashionable today,
I had cover-up tattoos done in Berlin which helped me accept mine in a way.

I regret not going to more football games and join in with the atmosphere,
My favourite team is Liverpool but have only managed one game over the years.
The opportunity was when a pre-season friendly brought 'the Reds' to Berlin in 1994,
Living abroad over half of my life is one excuse but nevertheless, I should see more.

Music; listening to music and going to concerts is another passion of mine,
I have a 'diverse' taste in music and have been to many concerts over time.
I was 12 when he passed but I still regret not seeing the 'King of Rock 'n' Roll,'
Elvis actually never performed outside North America anyway on the whole.
I listen to his music often and made a painting which hangs on my wall,
My first concert was 'Who's That Girl,' the 'Queen of Pop' and what a ball.
I regret not seeing the 'King of Pop,' he played in Berlin[2], I bet it was a thriller,
At least I saw George before he passed singing that 'Blair Bush[3]' song and 'Killer.'
I commemorate George and Michael with more of my works of art on my wall,
I was lucky enough to see Bon Jovi before and after Richie left when I recall.
I regret not seeing Freddy's *Queen*, George agrees that that man was somebody to love,
He rocked me, wanted it all and broke free, and now he bites the dust from above.
My favourite band is Nickelback and I am seeing them for the sixth time in May too,
We watched 'Take That' and 'Robbie' and will watch the group again in June.
I have U2, A-ha, Duran Duran, East 17, Kylie, Bruno and Lionel Richie under my belt,
I regret I didn't see Linkin Park before Chester Bennington died as sorrow was felt.
I regret not seeing 'The Script' before Mark Sheehan left us, life is so easy to lose,

'The Script' are carrying on and I will see them in the future which is good news.

After note from the poet; I eventually saw 'The Script' in Düsseldorf in December 2024.

---

[1] In my case (him).
[2] Where we were living at the time.
[3] Shoot the Dog—song by George Michael.

30. Family, A Short Story

My mother was the gentle one,
Mum was reserved and second to none.
I am my father's son,
Dad and I were very alike and I won.
I have only one sister and the best sister ever,
Unfortunately, we don't see each other often and I miss her.
I am my favourite brother's bro,
He is the only one who calls me 'Peggers,' you know.
The rest of the litter are out there somewhere,
And, I am so grateful that our siblings are all still here.

Firstly, our mum passed but I do talk to her at least every week,
When I do the chores and dust her picture and that's when I speak.
She was a *model* mother, a singer and a dancer,
What is sad is when I chat with her, she doesn't answer.

Secondly, our dad passed and I see him every day,
"How is that?" I hear you all say!
When I look in the mirror, he is there looking back,
He is probably reminding me to stand tall and never slack.
When I walk in the light of day, by me, his shadow is there,
With the same trait, bearing and gait, I walk his way and maybe unaware.
Unknowingly, we have the same military-drill-swinging-arms,
With that in common, we were proudly 'past meets present' brothers-in-arms.

We sadly lost our parted-parents who passed away in 2018,
They lived in the same town but unaware of each other it seemed.
Mum died first on Valentine's Day and Dad 3 months later in May,
They lived for nearly two centuries; "Hear, hear," we say.
Like I said earlier, I have a sister, my favourite and I love her,
She is the head of the estranged family and surely close we all once were.
I always joke and call her my favourite sister,

Even at our age, she always calls me her little brother.
She is the second oldest but definitely the anchor,
And for that reason and for many other reasons, I really appreciate her.
Separated by sea, but we are still very close and keep in touch,
For all her compassion throughout the years, "thank you very much."

Also mentioned above, one of my bros, my closest one of four,
I really wish that we could see each other more.
We too live in different countries and we don't see each other much,
Through email and conference calls, we try our best to keep in touch.
Again, like my dad, I look in the mirror and also see him,
In our senior years now and sort of retired, we are at our brim.
We too have much in common but it is not the bearing or gait,
Within these walls, I see him many times a day and a true mate.

Why do I <u>men</u>tion my dad and bro specifically?
Probably because we are/were so-alike, featurely.
This might be my interpretation and to the others, perhaps odd?
"Sadly, there is only us left now, bro, like 2 peas in a pod!"
Yes, I too boast about my one and only sister,
But in this particular verse, she is not a <u>mis</u>ter.

A husband and wife of over 36 celebrated years,
Not many can boast about that, so here are three cheers:
"Hurrah, hurrah, hurrah!"
My wife is steadfast, easy-going and fair,
When you need her, she will undoubtedly be there.
Parents to our 3 (now adult) children,
Some are separated by sea but we never need introduction.
They have collectively made us both very proud,
And for all their accomplishments, we shout out loud.
Doting love, marriage and partnership, none of us are alone,
We have grandchildren now; how much we have grown.
The soul-partners of our three, that they can't live without,
Embossed in each other and of that there is no doubt.

Epilogue

I would like to finish this book of poems with something colourful. I took up art at the age of about 41 and have completed over 100 exhibits of art thus far. The majority of them (which were given away as gifts) are simple paintings in acrylic. I started with horses then preferred abstract paintings. Of late, I have been painting/using 'air-freshener reed sticks' which turn into something quite magical. I include some of my favourite pieces here.

'Dam and Foal' for Vanessa.

'River Queen' for Yvonne.

'Ayden's Train.'

'Colour Design Black Gold 1' for Vanessa.

'Colour Design Black Gold 2' for Vanessa.

'Colour Design Black Gold 3' for Vanessa.

'Colour Design Black Gold 4' for Vanessa.

'Colour Design Black Gold 5' for Vanessa.

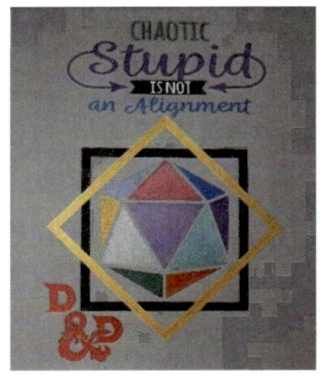

'D&D' for Tabea.

'Emotions' for Marion.

'Eye See Splendour' (Right 1/2) for Lisa.

'Felicidade' for the Portuguese Restaurant
Schwannenberg, Germany.

'A New Beginning' for Britta.

'Gefühle' (Feelings) for Britta.

(Oil) 'Heart' for Hannah.

'Brown Bear' for Lia.

'Love Dancing' for Marion.

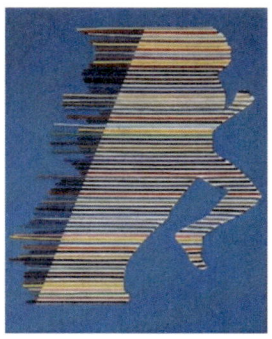

'Marathon Man' for Andrea and Jörg.

'Paris' for Frauke and Dennis.

'Port Ghalib.'

'Respect' for the neighbours.

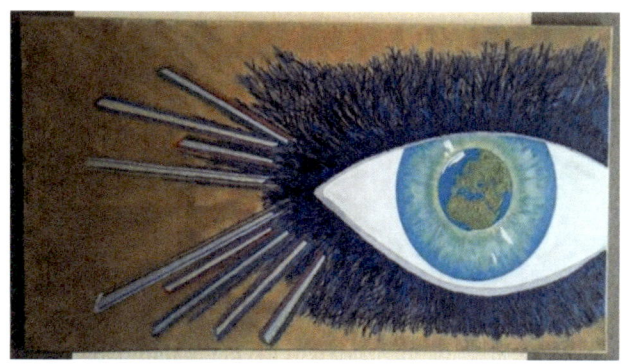

'See the World' for Gareth and Joan.

'Soul Window' for Vanessa.

'2 Face.'

Photograph of Neal (Warrant Officer Class Two in the Adjutant General's Corps (Staff and Personnel Support)). Neal's last position in the army was the Communications and Coordination Manager of the Media and Communications British Forces Germany Branch of the Joint Headquarters near Mönchengladbach, Germany, October 2011.

I am currently working on a second book and hope it will be published. A sort of part 2 to this book, carrying on with my autobiography with simple stories in my everyday life. Continuing my stories with poetry and sharing them with you. It is diverse, beautiful and a relatable perspective to readers. I write of favourite mega music icons who have died in my time, art, military discipline, celebration and keeping fit and I hope it resonates with you and gives you inspiration. I have finalised my list of poems and some of them are listed below.

- Watch and Shoot (a story about military shooting on the ranges).
- Take My Life, Take My Dreams, Take My Hand (a story about George Michael).
- Taking Care of Business (a story about Elvis Presley).

- Farewell My Summer Love (a story about Michael Jackson).
- Loser (a story about losing weight and fitness training at 59 all after a hip replacement which had to be changed again after just 1 year).
- Creatures Great and Small (a story about creatures (and things) at home and when we are out and about).
- A Symbol of Remembrance and Hope (a story/poem about The 'Red' Poppy and what it represents).
- Celebration on the Nile (a story about cruising the Nile).
- Military Discipline (a story about using it as a baseline in everything that you do.
- Olympics and Paralympic Games (a story about the history of the Olympics and Paralympic Games).
- What's in a Name? (a story about your given name(s)).
- 9 Lives (a story of managing to get out of difficult or dangerous situations without being harmed).
- Colours Are Brighter When The Mind Is Open (a story about taking up art at the age of 40+).
- Nelly Navel (a sort of funny Benjamin Button story).

Look after one another. Neal